Person to Person Managing

An Executive's Guide to Working Effectively with People

ALSO BY THOMAS L. QUICK

Your Role in Task Force Management:
    The Dynamics of Corporate Change
The Ambitious Woman's Guide to a Successful Career
    (with Margaret V. Higginson)
Understanding People at Work:
    A Manager's Guide to the Behavioral Sciences

Thomas L. Quick
Person to Person Managing

An Executive's Guide to Working Effectively with People

St. Martin's Press
New York

Library of Congress Cataloging in Publication Data

Quick, Thomas L
  Person to person managing.

  Includes index.
  1. Personnel management.   I. Title.
HF5549.Q52   658.3   76-62791
ISBN 0-312-60217-0

To Barbara Whitmore

and my Associate Membership colleagues

TABLE OF CONTENTS

Introduction   **xiii**

Chapter 1   **Pushing People's Buttons**   **1**
    Conveying your expectations   *1*
    Enhancing their motivation   *4*
    Setting significant goals   *5*
    Looking for the link   *8*
    Providing positive reinforcement   *9*
    Praising effectively   *11*
    Keeping partiality in its place   *12*
    Recognizing your key people   *16*
    Weeding out has motivational impact   *17*

Chapter 2   **Getting the News to—and from—**
   Employees   **21**
    Avoiding isolation   *21*
    Managing the news   *25*
    Measuring feelings about change   *27*
    Getting their ideas about yours   *29*
    Finding out what they think of you   *31*
    Hearing the feelings as well as the words   *34*
    Letting them talk   *37*
    Countering an attack by a subordinate   *38*

Chapter 3 **Managing Performance Problems**   **41**
    Confronting managerial obsolescence   *41*
    Correcting a faulty role perception   *45*
    Stimulating the on-the-job retiree   *47*
    Aiding recovery from a setback   *49*
    Working with an excusaholic   *53*
    Avoiding responsibility for alcohol problems   *55*

Chapter 4 **Dealing with Challenges to Your Leadership**   **59**
    Reinforcing the wrong image   *59*
    Toning down the temperamental wunderkind   *61*
    Looking beyond the continual complaints   *62*
    Dealing with defensiveness   *64*
    Feeling sensitive about humor   *67*
    Fending off others' work   *68*
    Integrating the employee with a past   *70*
    Deciding what to do about the office affair   *72*
    Handling an employee's personal problem   *74*

Chapter 5 **Getting Results Across Lines**   **77**
    Solving interdepartmental problems   *77*
    Being a graceful winner   *81*
    De-fanging the joking   *82*
    Putting down the put-down   *85*
    Dealing with the public attack   *88*
    Getting the attention of an unwilling audience   *90*
    Making a good partner   *93*

Chapter 6 **Working Effectively with Your Boss**   **97**
    Taking the measure of your boss   *98*
    Supporting your boss   *100*
    Praising the boss   *102*
    Getting the boss' attention   *103*
    Getting a bigger piece of the action   *106*
    Delegating to your boss   *107*
    Going up the line   *108*

Asking for a raise   *110*
Protecting yourself when you're a protégé   *113*
Looking good to the new boss   *115*
Being negative with the boss   *119*
Complaining to the boss   *121*
Protecting yourself in a conflict with the boss   *123*
Using clout   *124*

Chapter 7   **Dealing with Conflict**   **127**
Admitting conflict   *128*
Benefiting from conflict   *131*
Avoiding the suppression of conflict   *132*
Using the confrontation technique   *135*
Developing relationships by objectives   *136*
Deciding whether to intervene in a feud   *138*
Heading off an interdepartmental feud   *141*
Holding on to your scalp in others' conflicts   *142*

Chapter 8   **Countering Communications Problems**   **145**
Describing what you've seen   *149*
Learning from criticism   *150*
Mixing criticism with praise   *151*
Choosing the phone over the pen   *153*
Delivering the bad news   *155*
Sidestepping the put-down of another person   *155*
Choosing the place to talk to subordinates   *157*
Encouraging without promising   *159*
Giving the right impression in an interview   *160*
Using stress in interviews   *162*
Avoiding embarrassment in announcing a termination   *164*
Making noise about you   *165*
Planning a more effective presentation   *167*

Chapter 9   **Making Meetings More Productive**   **171**
Choosing the right size   *172*
Getting ideas on the table   *173*
Developing a good discussion   *175*

Making the decision stay decided   *176*
Using a group effectively   *179*
Shutting people off   *182*
Getting results from a committee you appoint   *183*

Chapter 10   **Standing Out in Meetings**   **185**
Observing the group process   *185*
Neutralizing the No   *192*
Pushing without dominating   *194*
Dealing with the hidden agenda   *196*
Helping the conference clam   *198*
Confronting the hog   *199*

Index   *203*

Person to Person Managing

An Executive's Guide to Working Effectively with People

Introduction

This book is about working with people—your subordinates, your fellow managers, the boss. In the end, everything you do in your work has to be done through and with people, and this book can help you do it more effectively.

Managing people isn't much of a science yet. We can develop symbols and equations for many financial, marketing, and production processes, but human relations are harder to classify. No two people, no two situations, are exactly alike. There is no one foolproof way to respond when you're asked for a raise. Nor is there one perfect formula for criticizing subordinates who make serious mistakes or turn in unsatisfactory work. You can't always take the same tone: with some people, you need to use almost authoritarian firmness, with others, a more relaxed approach.

But—even though there are no set formulas—management doesn't have to be trial and error. That is where this book comes in. By working through hundreds of interactions—examining what you might say or not say, do or not do in specific situations—the book can help sharpen your analytical skills. What is actually going on at this moment with this person? Why did the situation occur—and how can you stop it from recurring? What does the person need (which may be quite different from what he or she is asking for)? What do you need? What is the best answer for you, for the employee, for the organization?

One of the most important things this book can do is help you see and evaluate options. Are you stuck with the brilliant employee who makes trouble or the boss who takes over meetings? Or is there a new approach that can help? What about the chronic complainer, the excusaholic, the employee who drinks? What are your choices in the situation? And how can you judge which choice is most likely to be effective?

The guidelines and techniques in this book have been developed through the years by the professional staff of the Research Institute of America. These staff members, specialists in management and organizational behavior, study the techniques that successful managers use, seek out practical applications for research findings in the behavioral sciences, note virtually every book or article that has significance for managers, and evaluate all the trends. As a result, tens of thousands of executives every other week receive specific, pragmatic recommendations in *Personal Report for the Executive*, published by the Research Institute. Every year the report deals with hundreds of real problems, challenges, and opportunities that confront managers everywhere. And every year, the report grows more popular as it helps executive readers to become more effective managers, to get better results from their work with others. *Personal Report for the Executive* is probably the most widely circulated publication of its kind.

Those years of research and expertise have been packed into this book. It is an action tool for the results-minded executive.

chapter 1 Pushing People's Buttons

Managers continually ask the question, "How can I motivate my employees?" Actually, it's doubtful whether one person *can* motivate another. But it is undeniable that managers can influence, enhance, and help to unblock motivational forces in employees who report to them. That job is a highly complex one. As manager, you must be able to convey to employees your requirements or standards, and your expectation that they will meet these standards. Further, you must be able to set meaningful goals for employees, help make it possible for them to achieve these goals, and help make them want to achieve. You must be able to reward the performance you want, and take action with employees who cannot or will not meet your requirements.

Conveying Your Expectations

There is growing evidence, supported by psychological research, that a manager's expectation of subordinates' performance does indeed influence that performance. In other words, if you continually and convincingly act in a way that shows that you expect good work, you are more likely to get it than if your behavior suggests that you expect very little. There are at least four ways to tell your subordinates that you expect them to perform well:

Treat them with concern. If the work climate you establish is friendly, warm, supportive, trusting, and encouraging, then you are likely to see people trying to improve the quality and quantity of their work. It is important for subordinates to realize that you care about their needs and goals, that you want to help them find satisfaction on the job.

Employees today want bosses who act naturally rather than inspirationally, bosses who treat them as responsible adults. Unfortunately, there are still managers who feel they must constantly rekindle fires in their employees. Picture the manager who is always "up," booming confidence that all is well and going to get better. No one believes it. It is not a realistic, caring, person-to-person way of communicating.

Give help. Support people and help them to improve through teaching and by providing them with learning opportunities. Your actions can broadcast the message, "Look, I want you to be more effective in more situations," or "I want to make it possible for you to get more of the results you want in your work more of the time."

It is all too easy, however, to provide training in a way that underlines subordinates' deficiencies instead of their strengths, training that focuses entirely on overcoming weaknesses or faults rather than increasing strengths and existing talents. And in the case of high performers, it is easy to overlook the importance of continuing to provide special training. Continued training says, "You are capable of becoming even more effective than you are now," and suggests that you see employees as they see themselves. This will make them even more eager to achieve.

Be available to listen. Performance is more likely to improve if people feel free to ask what is expected of them. They need to know that they can turn to you for help without having it

held against them. "I am here to help you when you need me."
This continuing availability expresses confidence that
improvements will follow—and confidence influences
behavior. That way, learning becomes a continuing and
natural experience.

Show that you know what each employee is doing. When you
offer helpful criticism and reward accomplishment, you
answer each subordinate's unvoiced question, "How'm I
doing?" Whatever teaching you do may have little or no effect
unless the employee knows that you think the lesson has taken
hold—or that more practice is necessary.

This does not mean, however, that a manager can afford to
be unrealistic about subordinates' talents. Industrial psychologists say that if employees think the boss' expectations are
unrealistically high, their performance is unlikely to rise and
may even drop. This is the "what's the point of even trying"
phenomenon.

Thus, if you want more effective performance from those
who report to you, you must take these factors into
consideration:

Be sure that what you expect from subordinates is not more
than they can deliver by expending a reasonable amount of
effort—that is, usually without putting in extra hours and
enduring prolonged stress.

*Make clear to employees the difference between what you
require and what you expect.* They must understand what the
minimal acceptable level of performance is to meet the goals
you have established, as well as what you think they are
capable of accomplishing.

Allow for individual differences in ability and motivation.
Not everyone is going to meet the same standards, work at the
same pace, experience the same drive, or feel the same
commitment.

Exhibit a continuing desire and willingness to identify and
remove obstacles to employees' performance, such as

outmoded procedures, lack of knowledge and skill, poor supervision, and so on.

Your expectations of subordinates, however realistic, well-intentioned, and clearly communicated, are only the beginning. No doubt you've had the experience of trying to persuade an employee to take on a new assignment or to do a better job on the task the person was already responsible for. You were convinced the employee could do the job capably, only to find him or her reluctant or seemingly unable to live up to your expectations.

Enhancing Their Motivation
According to the social learning theory of Julian Rotter of the University of Connecticut, there are three significant factors involved in motivating a person to do a task: the value to the person of the work to be done or the thing to be achieved; the probability that he or she will be successful in doing or achieving it; and the situation in which it will be done or the circumstances surrounding the doing.

If you want to be reasonably sure, before you assign jobs or offer opportunities to subordinates, that they will be motivated to do good work, try to get answers to the following questions—and this usually means asking the employee.

Is this the kind of work the person would like to do? Will the National Accounts Manager really be interested in an assignment that would lead to the job of National Sales Manager? Is the Assistant Director of Engineering Services likely to feel that the path upward lies through taking over the function of materials management? Often people in positions of responsibility make the mistake of believing that whatever they think is of value, or whatever the organization labels as important, the subordinate should automatically want to do.

This is not always the case. The employee may not at first welcome the new assignment. But perhaps there are ways to make it seem more attractive: money, status, more desirable location, more advantageous career direction, a chance to shape the work or job.

Are there obstacles—if only in the person's mind—to doing the assignment well? If so, what would it take to increase the probability of success? You may want to offer training, experts to assist, or a new reporting setup. If success is not likely in employees' minds, they will not want to take on a job.

Would a change in the situation surrounding the work help? A different location, perhaps, or different people to work with? Perhaps the candidate for the position of Marketing Services Manager would view the job more favorably if she could have as her assistant someone on her present staff.

In short, when you take the trouble to find out how people really feel about their jobs, you can often help them to adjust comfortably and willingly to assignments and responsibilities that they might otherwise dislike or turn down. You might also uncover reasons why people are not performing well at present—and make changes.

Setting Significant Goals
Of course, in any endeavor, it is essential to have goals that people accept and toward which they can work. Goal-setting is, however, no simple task. One such method, known as *Management by Objectives* (MBO), has been gaining in popularity.

Here's how a typical MBO program might work. The operating head of a company or division sits down with immediate subordinates to work out specific objectives for the operation—to improve profit margins, to increase productivity, to strengthen competitive positions, etc. These goals are spelled out for a definite time period, say one year.

Each of the subordinates then gets together with his or her people to obtain their help in working out subgoals which collectively add up to the overall objectives. Preferably each manager sets the goals jointly with his or her immediate superior. For example, a production manager might work to increase profitability by cutting rejects from 7% to 5%. A sales manager might plan to add five salesmen to the present sales force by the end of a twelve-month period. The essential thing is that the goals must be specific, clearly understood, and agreed upon, so that the manager and his or her boss can measure the former's achievement during and at the end of the stipulated time.

In a working MBO program, goals are usually set on three levels: routine, problem-solving, and innovations.

Routine. At this level managers hope to improve the work they are already doing. For example, your department turned out 30,000 units last year. Without taking extraordinary steps, you aim for 33,000 units this year. Achievement of routine goals is not generally considered as a basis for incentive salary increases or promotions. The usual reward at this level has been expressed waggishly, "If you succeed, we'll let you keep your job."

Problem-solving. For example, absenteeism in a given department normally runs at 5% of the man-hours worked. It has jumped to 8%. By using tighter controls and closer supervision, the manager plans to get back to the lower rate.

Innovations. To set and achieve goals at this level requires creative effort. A financial manager might institute a bank draft system to improve cash flow. A marketing director plans to devise a more profitable product mix or even to introduce a new product line. A personnel or training manager outlines a new in-plant supervisory training program. A plant engineer designs a statistical quality control system.

But there is a fourth level too often ignored:

Personal development. This is probably the area of goal setting that is hardest to establish—and to measure. For one thing, career objectives may be difficult to express in annual units. Even so, the following questions can be asked of the subordinate in an annual goal-setting interview:

Where are you now? "Where" can be defined in terms of money, skills, achievement, kind of responsibility, education, etc. This question is primarily a prelude to the next.

Where would you like to be? It's useful to have a long-term view, but essential to have specific goals for the immediate future.

What are your plans for reaching your goal? The kind of education and training, schedule and mode of advancement, accomplishments, etc.

The subordinate may or may not be willing to discuss specific aspects of his or her personal development. But the goals should be set in the subordinate's mind. If he or she has thought out goals and directions and established ways to measure progress, then your final question becomes important and helpful:

How can I—and the organization—help you to reach your personal development goals? The resources you can supply can be discussed without the employee having to reveal what he or she regards as personally important. For example, you might describe some of the training and education programs available. Ideally, the employee should feel free to tell you what kind of thinking he or she has done about the first three questions. Obviously, however, if one of the answers to the question "Where would you like to be?" is, "I want to reach the point at which I can demonstrate I'm a better manager than you," then you can understand the employee's reluctance to level.

Of course, personal development is not confined to a formal education or training program. Behavior change is very important as well—to become, say, more of a negotiator, less of a rule-maker, with employees. The essential thing is that the employee recognize the desirability for some kind of progress and have a realistic idea how he or she plans to achieve that progress.

However, merely setting specific goals hardly guarantees that people will work to achieve them. Many MBO efforts fail. One of the most common reasons offered for the failure is top management's own failure to give strong support to the MBO program. Top management must define organizational goals in such a way that they can be broken down unit by unit, so that each individual can see what has to be done at his or her level to achieve the overall goals.

But as many managers have found, something is missing in this formula. For the individual employee, it is just not enough to see the relationship between one's own unit and overall organizational objectives. The employee has to see where his or her *personal* objectives fit in with organizational objectives in order to feel these organizational goals are worth working hard for.

Looking for the Link

How can you find out whether employees' personal objectives mesh with those of the organization? Sometimes you can tell by their obvious dedication to the formal goals, their enthusiasm in achieving them. But often you have to get answers to the following questions:

How important is the project or goal to them? Do they give the impression that it is high priority—or just another thing to be done? Do they think about how it is to be accomplished?

Do they feel optimistic about success? Do they have clear ideas as to what is required to make it possible? Do they feel that they can improve unsuccessful methods and procedures? Do you sense they are realistic in their planning? Is there considerable badmouthing or silence that could indicate pessimism?

What kind of contract do they have with you? If they do not object to a schedule by which the work and progress can be measured, then they are demonstrating a willingness to work with you. Do they accept the limitations of money, time, equipment, or staff that are imposed?

In your exchanges with the people who are going to do the

work, you can fairly well evaluate how personally important to them are the objectives that you consider in the best interests of you and the organization. The degree of their enthusiasm in taking on the work, of their involvement in planning how the work will be done, of their conscientiousness in trying to follow the schedule agreed upon—all these demonstrate to you how closely employees can identify with the objectives you want them to achieve. From these attitudes you can assess the amount of motivation in the people who report to you.

Providing Positive Reinforcement

When they work effectively, when they make satisfactory progress toward the objectives they've committed themselves to, you should make sure to reward them. Granted, they probably receive gratification from their achievements. But recognition of those achievements by you is probably at least as important to them. People work to gain recognition as much as to have a feeling of accomplishment themselves.

Enhancing the employees' satisfaction and feelings of accomplishment is only one reason to give rewards. You want a repetition of their effective behavior. More, you want—and presumably, so do they—even more effectiveness. So, as a manager, your recognition and rewarding of the behavior you want constitutes what psychologists call reinforcement—*positive reinforcement.*

The principle behind positive reinforcement, a concept closely associated with Harvard psychologist B. F. Skinner, is this: specific behavior in others can be encouraged and shaped. It's a school of thought that frightens some people, who associate it with Pavlov's dogs, or with pigeons pecking at levers to get food.

Behavior conditioning, however, is not a mindless process. A person's behavior is influenced by what that person perceives as the consequences of his or her behavior. When an employee passes the president of the company in the hall, the subordinate isn't likely to trip the senior executive. The consequences of such an act would be too painful (for both of them). The consequences of being respectful could be rewarding. The same applies to more complicated situations.

A second factor in positive reinforcement is that another person is involved. That other person, usually a manager, is the one who defines the desired behavior and is also the person responsible for rewarding it when it occurs.

Here's how one behavioral scientist demonstrates to executives the effectiveness of positive reinforcement.

One executive in the group is asked to leave the room. While he or she is out, a task is selected—for example, to touch the shoulder of a particular person in the room. The executive is called back and told that he or she must do something. But the person isn't told what.

The psychologist has one hundred pennies and a cup before him. When the subject makes a move in the right direction (toward the person whose shoulder is to be touched), the psychologist drops a penny into the cup. When the subject makes a wrong move, there is only silence. Usually, before the supply of pennies is used up, the subject will learn—and do—what is expected.

In day-to-day management, when the stakes are higher, positive reinforcement will work the same way, provided you make sure to observe the following conditions:

Explain the behavior you want to the person. The employee is to sell more of Product A, to cut costs by 18%, or to solve some nagging problem. Let him or her know the consequences of success (approval, more money, promotion, the esteem of others, etc.).

Give feedback—reinforce—while the person is trying to change the behavior. Reinforce the specific act or accomplishment and offer the reinforcement as soon as possible after it occurs, so that the person relates your reinforcement to the program. ("You really are coming along faster than I expected.")

Be consistent. Unfortunately, we give conflicting signals. We tend to forget to reinforce, and the other person may begin to feel that what we're asking is not important after all, or that even a good performance will not be rewarded. Thus, until the new behavior becomes a pattern, find ways to comment on it regularly. Show the person that you're observing it and that you're pleased by it. The point to remember—and this is where many managers fail—is that where significant behavior change is required, reinforcement is not a one-shot or occasional thing—it must be repeated.

Don't emphasize the negative side. If you've embarked on a program of positive reinforcement, try to soft-pedal the negative. If the employee's failures or slips are not major, it might be best to ignore them so as not to detract from the positive accomplishments.

Praising Effectively
One reason why positive reinforcement is not as widely applied as it could be is that it's deceptively simple. It's so simple, in fact, that many people find it hard to believe it can actually change behavior.

Rewards or reinforcements are essential. And they should be meaningful to the employee. A meaningful reward enhances the value of the task or function. The reward many managers immediately think of is money, which in most organizations is the reward that's least available. Managers are restricted by budgets that limit not only the amount of money they can use as a reward, but the occasions when they can offer it. Reinforcers that come only once a year are not terribly effective.

A reward that is available in unlimited quantities is praise. It is remarkably effective as a reinforcer when used sensitively and skillfully. If praise is to accomplish what you want it to, though, it can't be dispensed carelessly. There are certain factors to consider:

Mean what you say. This is the critical factor for all praise. If an accomplishment is not praiseworthy in your opinion, and you praise it anyway, you'd have to be a pretty exceptional actor to keep an employee from seeing through the phony words. What will probably go through the employee's mind is "Does the boss think I'm slipping? Or that this is all I'm capable of?"

Say exactly what you mean; don't "shovel it on." A sales rep who has been in a slump sells a moderately good account, nothing spectacular. The sales manager says, "Great job." But the employee has a hard time figuring out what is meant. Had the sales manager said something like, "I'm glad you sold Dalton. It came at a good time for you," he would have been expressing exactly what he meant, and would have been entirely believable.

Employees are understandably resentful when praise is too effusive—it's an insult to their abilities and intelligence.

Praise should be appropriate to the achievement. An accomplishment may be worthy of recognition, but a few words may be all that's needed to give that recognition. For example, "That was a very good memo you sent me yesterday, and it's helpful to me to have it."

Strike a balance. Since praise is a form of recognition, it should be given often enough to keep employees from feeling that their efforts are futile. On the other hand, praise that comes so regularly as to be almost predictable has little impact.

The tricky thing is that the right timing will change. Employees new to a task may need frequent recognition as they master various aspects of the job. As they progress, however, they not only do not need such frequent praise, they don't deserve it. The accomplishments that were originally praiseworthy have now become routine.

Keeping Partiality in its Place

For a manager to show favoritism toward a subordinate is wrong. Right?

That's what a lot of managers have always heard. Yet favored treatment has its place, if it is wisely used. Many executives are coming to feel that favors and extraordinary privileges can be used to reward outstanding service instead of (or in addition to) money, promotion, or other traditional rewards. What distinguishes this kind of favoritism from the kind that has generally been regarded as bad management practice? Special treatment used as a reward is not based on personal likes or dislikes, or seniority or position in the organizational hierarchy. It is based on performance. It is earned by the subordinate, not gratuitously bestowed by the manager. Above all, it is given in recognition of past and current proven worth, not in anticipation of the future.

The manager who favors an employee to show faith in that person's potential is simply asking for trouble. What people with unproven abilities need is the chance to show what they can do.

On the other hand, as the research of psychologist Frederick Herzberg shows, employees whose achievements win recognition are motivated to keep up the good work. The accent is on achievement, however, and favored treatment should be given as a reward for consistent high performance, not for one outstanding piece of work.

If you take the time to make a list, you may be surprised at the variety of non-monetary ways to show valued employees—and others—how highly you regard solid, sustained contributions. Generally these "substitutes" provide growth and advancement opportunities and enable an employee to gain greater satisfaction from his or her work. Perhaps you can use one or more of these methods to reward someone to whom you can't give more money at the moment:

More independence. This means more than reducing the amount of checking up and directing you do. Let exceptional performers have more to say about their own conduct and activities. You may even suggest that they try to redesign their jobs to allow them to spend more time doing what they enjoy doing, whatever gives them the most sense of achievement. You may be able to show them how to delegate the portions of their job that provide the least satisfaction; perhaps others can do these as well. Or you may reassign some of the less satisfying duties to others who would get more gratification from handling them.

Letting certain employees plan and schedule their own work may involve some risk. And the changes they initiate may lead to no appreciable difference in output. Still, it's a psychological lift, as well as a sign that they merit special consideration.

More authority. One reward that managers don't give often enough is work that they themselves enjoy doing. But now, when you are looking for ways to keep valuable people satisfied, is the time to delegate certain jobs that are important to you. Make sure these jobs are challenging and offer them opportunities to grow. Otherwise, the person you're trying to reward may get the feeling you're dumping more work on him or her without any additional compensation. For your part, you are making a sacrifice, giving up what you like to do. But it is an investment that could pay handsome dividends.

Varied responsibilities. Another form of reward is to let outstanding workers pass on their skills by breaking in new employees, taking much of the responsibility for their orientation. Or let them help upgrade present employees. Be careful, however, that working with less skilled employees does not seem to be a demotion. Make it clear to the persons to whom you give the task that they are actually taking over one of your responsibilities, and that you are giving them the assignment because you recognize their talents.

Another way to reward competence is to let the high achievers bring their experience to bear on organizational problems that they weren't privy to in the past. Chances are you need all the experienced help you can get. Within your own area especially, ask for their opinions and ideas. Let them do some background research for new plans, changes in procedures, etc. Their participation can relieve you of some of the responsibility you have been carrying alone.

Learning. You can help good workers increase their worth to the organization—and their self-worth. If your budget permits, you may want to send them to a seminar or course that could promote their career and salary advancement. So long as people don't have the feeling they are just standing still, they are less likely to be resentful or to look for bigger and better opportunities in another company.

The above are major forms of recognition. There are many more, perhaps not so substantial. For example:

Compensatory time (for personnel exempt from wage and hour laws). Your response to requests for time off should vary considerably—more relaxed and more generous with people who perform well than with those whose output is less commendable or merely minimally acceptable.

A trip. Suppose the branch office in Denver needs a few days of your time. At least, you are the person who has always gone. But couldn't Anne—who has just completed a tough assignment—handle the job almost as well? And might the trip not be useful in developing her potential for future assignments?

Visibility. People whose work you appreciate will probably value any recognition you arrange from higher-ups. After a particularly demanding assignment, you might see that they get individual memos from a top executive telling them that you mentioned the fine job they did.

More of your time. Try allocating more of your time for the people whose performances stand out. Casual chats, asking their opinion of certain projects, informal coaching to help them develop their potential—all can be used to signal your approval. And by visiting their offices or desks instead of having them come to your office, you give visible evidence of your special interest in high performers.

Other perquisites that may be used as rewards are: books or subscriptions to relevant periodicals; special stationery; a redecorated office (or one in a more desirable location); chairing meetings you'd normally head; periodic chances to work at home; a request that the subordinate take customers or other outsiders to lunch.

When you think about it, there are any number of ways, large and small, that you can clearly demonstrate how you value outstanding performance. And you don't have to break your budget to do it.

Some managers are reluctant to use favors as rewards because they are afraid they'll stir up a hornets' nest of grumbling, jealous employees. If this happens, you should ask yourself why the grumblers don't realize you are rewarding superior performance. Such grousing is usually a clear sign either that your performance standards are not understood or that you are rewarding only one type of achievement, thus cutting off those who don't excel in that particular field. If an individual has genuinely earned a reward because of sustained good work, as measured by clear standards, his or her colleagues will recognize that fact just as well as you do.

Recognizing Your Key People

Most managers realize they have to fight biases all the time. Special rewards such as we've talked about can be justified as a recognition of superior performance. Sometimes, however, they are extended to an employee whose performance doesn't justify it. In that case, the manager may have a special fondness for the employee, or exaggerate that person's potential (which somehow doesn't quite get realized).

On the other hand, managers, perhaps because of personal reasons ("She's a good worker, but I can't stand her"), will often overlook exceptional performance by certain people. Or they may take those people for granted, assuming the employees realize how they are valued, while extending favors to others.

In order to evaluate your own judgment about people, you should ask yourself several questions. How do your subordinates feel about their importance? Are you sure that those who are important to you, and to the organization, know it? Whom do you consider the cornerstones of your group? Undoubtedly several names immediately pop into mind. But can you be sure of your instant evaluation?

Here's a way of finding out just how vital each person is. Make a list of all the people who report to you and/or who work for your subordinate managers. Then, for each name on the list, ask yourself the following questions:

What does this person do that no one else does? Or at least no one else does quite as well, or as often.

What does this person do better than anyone else? It can be just as useful to record high-level skills and performance even if they are not necessarily unique.

What would happen if this person stopped doing the job? Perhaps the gap could be filled by others. Then again, while the work would get done, perhaps it wouldn't be done as well by someone else.

Who else's work depends upon this person? Here you have to think about quantity as well as quality. If someone else were to take over and do less work, or work of lesser quality, how would that affect other people?

As you probe for the answers to these questions relative to each name on your list, you may be newly impressed with the essentiality of each. But this recognition is only the start. Now ask yourself another question:

Does each person know—is he or she told periodically—the answers I found to the above questions? When each person feels like a cornerstone of the organization, that feeling has a positive effect on his or her motivation.

You may find to your surprise that an employee you have always regarded as a cornerstone doesn't fare so well by comparison with others on your list. Perhaps your previous evaluation needs reconsidering.

Weeding Out Has Motivational Impact
What about the people who do not produce according to your expectations and standards? Some managers say there will always be a curve with some performers at the lower end. No

matter what the manager does to provide the right climate for
motivation and individual excellence, there will be those who
will not respond. Why not get rid of them?

Many a manager is looking for excuses to avoid firing
anyone these days. Compassion is a strong motive, though not
the only one. When the economy is uncertain, executives are
always inclined to avoid any unsettling changes because of
their effect on work force morale.

Keeping people who are a known quantity has other
advantages, too. The present team is predictable, even if it
includes substandard performers. Managers and team
members alike know its dynamics. Introduce one or more
new people into the department and you have a different ball
game. Furthermore, new entrants need orientation, and that
slows the pace and makes demands on time that is already
short.

All these are valid reasons for the executive to hold onto a
group that isn't the best or the most effective. They are
particularly compelling when you feel you are throwing
someone to the wolves because jobs are so hard to find.

There is another side to these arguments, however. How do
the people who work with the inferior performers feel?

These days most people tend to believe that sooner or later
they will be asked to assume more work, as usually happens
during times of crisis. The extra burden will be far more
onerous than necessary when some team members don't carry
a fair share, and get away with it.

Most important, the fact that you put up with people who
don't work up to standards can erode the effectiveness of your
reward system. You lose credibility when you say that what
counts is good work, yet you tolerate poor workers.

What you need is a program that gives you the flexibility to
upgrade staff without subjecting yourself or the entire group
to unneeded stress. Some steps to consider:

A continuing clear statement of what is expected. One
managerial function is to set performance standards and
goals. Sometimes, however, these are referred to only
haphazardly, either because overall performance is high or

because the manager assumes that employees know what is expected of them and what will not be tolerated. But they may not. If standards and goals have not been stressed regularly, now is the time to reestablish them and be sure that everyone, no matter how satisfactory a performer at present, understands them clearly.

Notice to those employees whose performance is below the minimum standard. Once again, a manager may assume that employees who face the risk of termination know it, but that isn't necessarily so. Furthermore, substandard employees deserve to have specifics about what is wrong with their work—too many absences, inadequate skills for part of the job, goals that haven't been met, etc. Be sure to give specific examples in the event an employee feels he or she has received unjust, discriminatory treatment.

A reasonable probation period after notice. During this period the employee should be expected to improve performance. The individual should be provided with specific guidance and opportunities to acquire or sharpen the requisite skills. If there is little or no improvement at the end of the period, notice of termination should come as a matter of course, without surprise and with sufficient documentation.

Letting everyone know where he or she stands has a substantial impact on how subordinates respond to you. When you follow a consistent program of rewarding good performance and replacing those employees who cannot perform adequately, you will have little trouble convincing employees that you can provide a working climate that will enhance their self-images and help them fulfill their personal objectives.

chapter 2 Getting The News To —and From— Employees

What goes on between your subordinates and you? Do you really know? Do they communicate with you? To be effective, you need to know what employees know, think, wonder about. You need to know how they see you. You can expect to get the truth only when employees trust you and accept the fact that it is in their and your best interests to be honest with you. They have to feel comfortable in leveling with you, and confident that you will be fair in your reception of information—that you will not punish or discriminate against them because they tell you what you would prefer not to hear.

When you maintain wide open channels of communication, you risk hearing not only news you wish you didn't have to hear but the feelings of subordinates as well. You can't shut off the flow every time something unpleasant comes along.

Avoiding Isolation
All too frequently, sometimes without knowing it, a manager conveys to employees what information he or she expects to

hear and what should not come to the manager's desk. Sometimes the manager practically says, "I dare you to tell me anything."

There are executives who seem to feel that it is a subordinate's responsibility to beat down the boss' door, rather than the boss' responsibility to make sure that urgent information gets through. Perhaps unconsciously, some managers project the idea that subordinates must convince them of their right to be heard.

Such managers can find themselves lamenting more and more frequently, "Why wasn't I told?" Yet at the same time they may fail to realize that their own behavior may be the reason no one is bringing them essential information.

What you know determines what you do. It's part of your job to be sure you have any communication that will aid you in planning and decision-making, and to learn what is going wrong while there is still time to do something about it. Executives who act on the basis of inexact or incomplete information run risks they would never take if they had all the facts. Many times they discover too late that someone down the line did have the information, but failed to pass it along.

Some employees never volunteer data because keeping it to themselves makes them feel indispensable. For example, a newly appointed division head brought in from the outside discovers that one subordinate with some thirty years' experience is a repository of knowledge about the operation that cannot be found in formal records. The senior employee is quite happy to impart this knowledge, but only on his own terms: bit by bit, in carefully managed segments and only when sought out by the boss. He literally forces his superior to come to him.

It's far more common, however, to see managers unwittingly encourage subordinates to keep things from them. In one large corporation, three separate field sales groups were consolidated under one vice president. Before the consolidation, the expense and cost policies and methods for each group had been different. The vice president brought in a young consultant to establish one uniform cost and expense method.

The director of sales, who reported to the vice president, was concerned because the consultant seemed totally insensitive to what the three field sales managers thought of the proposed changes. Twice the sales director tried to warn the vice president about the grumbling he heard. The result? He was told that he was not giving the younger man a chance, that his negative attitude was infecting the field managers.

After that, the sales director withheld further evidence and eventually two valued field managers quit in disgust. Only then did the vice president realize how demoralized his field management staff had become. Like many other executives, he had cut himself off from getting vital information in time by his reaction to a candid, negative opinion. Without meaning to, he had said, in effect, "If you do this thing one more time, you'll regret it."

The higher an executive goes, the more likely it is that isolation will become a problem. Subordinates have a stake in controlling who and what reaches the boss; that's how they show their value. And the harassed executive appreciates being protected from trivia and time-wasting details. At the same time, though, it's easy to forget that the barrier may intimidate people who should get through in special circumstances.

As an executive, your goal should be to have a system which doesn't encourage bypassing the barrier, but doesn't eliminate the possibility. Striking a balance between too much openness and not enough often requires a difficult adjustment. These measures, however, may help:

Recheck your screen. Talk to your secretary and assistants, the layers of management beneath you. Let them know that there are sound reasons to limit access to you, but that there will be exceptions, too. Perhaps it is better to risk occasional unnecessary interruptions than to risk complete isolation. You also have to check from time to time what your trusted assistants have decided not to bother you with. Asking occasionally what they know but you don't will emphasize the importance you place on information—good *and* bad.

It can also be worthwhile checking further. Do employees

think you will be annoyed at their "wasting" your time if they come to you directly with something they believe important? If so, they won't storm the gates when they ought to.

Make a point of keeping in touch. You can find ways to chat occasionally with people who don't usually have access to you—in person if possible, by phone if that's not convenient. Say, for example, that a subordinate who reports to one of your assistants is assigned a project in which you are particularly interested. When the project is assigned, at least once while it's in progress, and at the end would be appropriate occasions for you to talk to the subordinate—and not necessarily just about the matter at hand.

Reward, don't punish, the messenger. You can hardly be blamed for reacting to unpleasant news. But there is a perceptible difference between gnashing your teeth over a problem and taking your anger out on the person who reported it. Whether the news is bad or good, the person bearing the news should receive appreciation and recognition.

Remember that employees may not feel that it is their responsibility to go to any unusual effort to bring urgent information to your attention. They have to *want* to do it. And you, of course, have a great deal to do with that. Employees will help you if they feel that you value their frankness and that you won't punish them. Be sure to thank them for their effort. You don't have to show immense gratitude. A simple expression of appreciation for their alertness will do.

The extent to which you show that you value employee initiative in bringing you information will aid you in meeting a problem many managers experience: hearing from those who are brash and assertive, but not from others who have news but won't push themselves through your door. You don't necessarily want to shut off the more assertive employees, unless they lose credibility or become a major nuisance. You do want to encourage the less assertive person by perhaps showing extra appreciation and, if possible, publicizing how much you valued his or her coming forward.

Employees may sometimes report information that they regard as urgent and you do not. Stifle your irritation, unless it is someone who carelessly brings unchecked data or a person bearing scurrilous tales.

Frown on lapses in information. When people admit that they didn't keep you informed, let them know that you don't want this kind of "protection." A couple of strong reactions by a manager, and a subordinate learns to make sure the boss gets the word—all of it.

Suspect good news from an interested source. If you've handed a tricky assignment to a subordinate and get nothing but rosy reports of progress, poke into the situation a bit more. Ask other people who are involved how things are going. Or play the devil's advocate and ask about problems you can imagine arising. Your subordinate may be reluctant to bring them up without encouragement.

Watch your body language when you hear bad news. If you always listen with an abstract air when hearing something you'd rather not, the message will get across. Then it won't be long before people will tell you only the things they know will arouse your enthusiasm. Similarly, if you associate some individuals with bad news and show that you dislike conversing with them, they will start keeping away—and let you stay uninformed.

Managing the News
Among the ways a manager can convey the impression to employees that the truth, the whole truth, and nothing but the truth is not really wanted is the let-there-be-happiness message that dictates there will indeed be happiness—or else. Unfortunately, some managers fall into the trap of saying all is well and then assuming that it actually is.

One sales manager announced a new campaign premium for distributors to increase sales. He wrote to his district managers, "I know you'll agree that this can really help us move the GFX line. I'm very anxious to hear from you as to how you've used it successfully."

Five managers out of 25 wrote to tell him the new campaign was great. Forgetting that this was all the feedback he had asked for, the sales manager concluded that the campaign was an unqualified success, that the other 20 salespeople felt the same way. In reality some didn't; they felt that the premium program discriminated against certain kinds of dealerships.

This example illustrates some common pitfalls in communications—pitfalls rooted in human nature itself:

It is hard to determine the dividing line between being positive and dictating the kind of response you expect.

We tend to listen to only what we want to hear, and to head off what we don't want to hear.

Others, especially subordinates, tend to tell us what they think we want to hear and to conceal what they believe we don't want to hear.

Managers who don't remain aware of these pitfalls are fooling themselves. They frame verbal and written statements to get the response they want. Then, having gotten it, they interpret the feedback as objective and as representing a consensus.

Of course, human nature being what it is, even the most conscientious manager will find it difficult to admit that he or she is conditioning the feedback. But by observing a few simple recommendations managers can at least reduce the danger that they will hear only what they want to hear.

Get timely participation. Encouraging feedback in the formative stages of a project (for example, during preparation of a product or planning a meeting) increases the chance that you will get an accurate reading of how subordinates feel about it. Getting their suggestions before you make your decision doesn't prevent you from "preserving your options," and furthermore, you have a better chance to get their genuine acceptance when you do make the final decision.

Don't oversell. It is understandable that you are pleased with the new product, the meeting, the new fringe benefits, but you don't really have to use superlatives like "best," "most up-to-date," "far ahead of competition." Nor do you have to pat yourself and the company on the back by saying, in effect, "Haven't we done a wonderful job?" or "We've done something we can all be proud of."

Don't demand agreement. Simple and common phrases such as "As you know," and "I'm sure you'll agree" often betray the writer's fear that people don't know or won't agree.

Leave time for reevaluation. Professional writers know the danger of unwittingly projecting their own views and biases too strongly into what they're writing. One way to test copy is to let it lie in the drawer for a few days, then take it out and read it with a fresh eye. Embarrassing or compromising excesses will then be more readily discernible.

Measuring Feelings about Change

A similar management of feedback frequently occurs after a manager makes some sort of change. It could be that he has introduced an open-door policy, urging employees with whom he once had little contact to come to him directly. Or maybe she has just had the office renovated. Now, she notes contentedly, her subordinates and the clerical staff are placed to encourage a logical work flow, with fewer distractions. Or possibly he or she has introduced staggered work hours in an effort to help the municipal traffic problem. Or restructured a lot of boring jobs—small wonder, the manager thinks, that productivity was low before!

Whatever the innovation, the boss' contentment is unmistakable. But is it catching?

Not necessarily. True, there are accommodating smiles each time he or she remarks on how much better things are now. True, there is not a word of complaint or criticism. But that doesn't mean that the supervisors who feel bypassed under the new open-door policy aren't smoldering. Or that all those people who have been moved around or put on different hours or given more responsibilities, or whatever, *like* the changes that have been introduced.

Sudden changes in behavior or policy often create anxiety and suspicion. Usually people can resolve such feelings by going to the boss and talking them out. But when they are reacting to a change he or she has introduced, people will sometimes tend to conceal any negative feelings they may have. They may have fears about the reasons for the change. And they don't want to have them confirmed by the boss.

Take, for example, the men and women supervising rank-and-file employees who are now encouraged to talk directly to a higher executive. To supervisors, an open-door policy almost inevitably brings fears that the executive in question may think they haven't been reporting accurately. Rather than risk finding out that their fears are well-grounded, they will grin and bear the new procedure, and try to conceal their distress.

When the manager is obviously satisfied and pleased with the change, no one wants to destroy the boss' good mood or, in particular, be the first to knock the project. Yet underneath the smooth surface there may be all sorts of problems that eventually the manager will have to deal with. These will probably grow more severe the longer they fester unheeded.

It is not enough for a manager to explain to the people affected the benefits of a change as the manager sees them. He or she must make sure that the benefits are actually being achieved. The only way to do that is to get honest reactions from those involved. Here are several approaches that will help you get just that:

Give every change a trial period, and label it as such. If people think you are not yet totally committed, that your mind is still open to suggestions, they will be more likely to level with you. "Let's try to see if it works" is a better approach than the flat edict.

Check back with people at reasonable intervals. Don't mix your question with a lot of other matters that obscure your desire for feedback.

Don't ask people if they like the change, but specifically how it has affected their work. *Yes* or *no* doesn't tell you much.

Where change is involved, no news is *not* good news. The manager must know how the new procedure is being received by the people involved. The only way to find out is from them.

Getting Their Ideas about Yours

Even when managers honestly seek subordinates' views on new projects, they often get "yes-yes" responses. For some people, the fact that it's the boss' plan turns a suggestion into a sacred cow.

What makes a subordinate keep silent when he or she considers the boss' proposals second-rate or even potentially disastrous? Employees may tell themselves that they don't like to rock the boat. They may say they don't want to get into a hassle. Their real motive, however, is fear of offending someone who holds the key to the future. Self-protection is the name of the Tactful Silence game.

Problems are bound to spring up when a less-than-good idea makes the grade simply because it's your brainchild. All too often, you are so close to your ideas that you can't judge them objectively. For your own self-protection, you should seek the honest opinion of others.

How, though, can you be sure you're getting the real thing? Some of the factors involved in getting honest opinions from subordinates are the same as in avoiding isolation in general:

Make sure of your motives. Do you truly want the other person to level with you? Are you prepared to listen to adverse comments without becoming defensive or tuning them out? Managers must send out clear signals that they are interested in the minuses as well as the pluses. Understandably, few subordinates are willing to stick out their necks if they sense their boss wants uncritical approval.

This doesn't mean that you can't indicate you think your idea is good. Yet by asking how your plan can be improved, you avoid tipping the scales. One possible approach is, "You can help me a great deal on this, Joe. I'd like to get any suggestion you have." Another might be, "This is a bit rough. I have a feeling I haven't touched all the bases." Joe then doesn't get the feeling he has to come out with a flat good/bad verdict.

Avoid a fait accompli aura. Timing always makes a difference. Asking for an opinion when it's almost too late to make changes in a proposal more or less guarantees receiving a "Great, boss" response. The same holds true if you ask for subordinates' views a half hour before you are scheduled to present the plan to higher management.

People are generally loathe to make changes in what seems like the final version of a plan. It's a good idea to let subordinates see it before the final typing stage. Providing copies typed with extra-wide margins encourages them to jot down their comments.

Get two or more heads. Ask for more than one opinion, and let each person know you're asking others. This will encourage honesty, because each person will know that the onus isn't all on him. And each may be eager to show that he or she is as smart as the other person.

Dig deeper. In most instances, it takes more than a "What do you think?" to get the full story. To accept the other person's opinion without probing to find the basis for it and asking for elaboration is to cut off a promising source of ideas.

Your tone of voice and facial expression can be all-important here. If you appear at all defensive or impatient, you won't get any further useful response. An over-aggressive reaction, such as "I don't understand what you're saying! Tell me exactly what you're driving at," can shut off the flow of words as effectively as an open threat.

You may already have thought through all the possible defects a subordinate brings up, or have considered and already rejected the suggestions offered. Often it seems a waste of time to explore them once again. Yet how much honest feedback you get in the future depends on your attitude and patience now.

Given the natural reluctance of subordinates to criticize the boss (any boss), it's only to be expected that creating a climate of openness is a never-ending job.

Finding Out What They Think of You

It's one thing when you encourage subordinates' opinions of something specific you have done or are planning to do. Many executives do spend a fair amount of time trying to keep up with employees' opinions about what is going on in their operations. Far fewer managers make a consistent effort to include in that information what employees think of the managers themselves.

One manager had this brought home to him somewhat unpleasantly in a conversation with an assistant, who was lunching with him on her last day in the department. She was being promoted and transferred to another division.

The manager began to describe how he believed in delegating widely, his insistence upon decentralizing decision-making responsibility, how fervently he believed in providing an open, supportive atmosphere in which people could communicate freely and develop their skills. It wasn't high-flown rhetoric. His description was low-key, matter-of-fact. No wonder, then, that he was thrown off balance when his assistant said, also matter-of-factly, "I've been debating whether I should tell you this. And I hope you won't consider me unkind. I know you see yourself as you've described. But this is not how many people in the department look at you. I get the impression that you must impose your values and perspective on those who work for you. You come across as very intolerant—and rather arbitrary. You say 'do this' in an absolute manner one week, and do a turnabout the next."

Unsettling—yes. But no one can long operate effectively without getting feedback from others as to how his or her behavior is seen by them. Conditions change, people change, goals change—and so does behavior. In the case of this manager, the disparity between how he thought he acted and how others saw him was not an instance of elaborate self-deception. In his early days as a manager, he had in fact been far more open. He had been inexperienced, unsure, and had done a better job of bringing employees into decisions, letting them have more say in the operation. Then, as his responsibilities increased, as his confidence in his managerial ability grew, and as his success became indisputable, his way of acting toward employees changed. They were aware of the change, but he wasn't. Primarily he didn't know it because he no longer enjoyed the kind of feedback he had once had.

How about the information you get from the people who report to you?

Do you solicit feedback—or want to receive it? Obviously it's not as simple as asking, "How do you see me?" Or, "How do you feel about the action I took?" The point is that managers really have to make it known how much they value the answer to that question. If the manager waits for it, and receives little, there is the temptation to believe things are fine.

Do you listen more to some people than to others? Most people would not go to their worst enemies to get an objective evaluation of their own effectiveness. And most would not go to an ardent admirer. Nonetheless, everyone places more credence in the opinions of some people than others. Some employees are more intelligent and/or articulate than others. Executives prefer talking with those with whom they are comfortable. All these preferences have some bearing on the things they *expect* to hear.

It is easy, very human, to maintain open channels of communication with some people but not with others, and to assume that you are not being selective so much as random, when you are not being random. There may be a number of reasons why you have not heard from particular people in your department for a time, but it is always wise to suspect your biases and self-protective tendencies.

Do you listen, or do you explain? For example, one employee comes to you with a complaint that other employees have received preferential treatment, and spells out what she means. You recognize that the employee has a different perspective on the situation than you do, so you hasten to explain things she doesn't know. You see it as an opportunity to give her information.

But you may not be hearing all of what she may be trying to tell you. She may be prepared to give you more feedback if you prove receptive—which you do not. She may be the only vocal employee of several, and your reply to her does not correct the similar "misimpressions" of others. On a long-range basis, you may discourage her from trying to talk about departmental conditions again. "What's the use? The boss doesn't really listen. He just gets defensive."

It might be more helpful to listen without challenging or correcting, and to to ask such questions as, "Do you think others in the the department have this viewpoint?" "Have you seen other instances of what you regard as preferential treatment?" Then say you'd like to think over what she has said, that you'll get back to her.

Do you check out with others what you've heard from one person? A general sort of question such as "Do you think morale has fallen lately?" probably won't get much response, but you may open all sorts of doors by saying, "Someone came to me the other day to say . . . ; do you think that condition exists?" Or, "Have you noticed that sort of thing?"

Do you ever try to isolate people who give you unpleasant feedback? If the person is not someone you admire strongly or whose credibility is always high, you may conclude that the unwelcome comments represent only an eccentric view. Yet this is not necessarily the case. You have no way of finding out if you refuse to listen, or do not check how others feel.

In such situations, some managers will try to put the employee on the defensive. Some will discount what was said, possibly commenting to others that the employee in question has once again shown poor judgment—a sure way to discourage honest comments.

Over a period of time many people become quite skilled in matching their perceptions of how they behave with the image they want others to have of them. Anyone who takes a contrary view is just not heard. The only way to avoid this unrealistic bind is to be sure the lines of communication are open to critics as well as supporters.

Hearing the Feelings as Well as the Words

Consider this scenario. A manager's assistant complains that his salary is too low. Surprised, the manager points out that the assistant got a substantial raise only six months ago, even though, because of an economy drive, most employees had had salaries frozen temporarily or had received only token raises. Trying not to act annoyed, the manager explains further that the assistant's salary is now the highest in the department (except for the boss's), that, considering the assistant's experience and seniority, his pay is comparable to that of other people at his level in the company. Furthermore, it is competitive with the salary offered in other companies for the kind of work he is doing.

The assistant leaves the manager's office, obviously unconvinced. Such illogical behavior, thinks the manager.

But there isn't really anything necessarily logical or illogical in the behavior. The fact is that most human behavior is *non-logical*—it is motivated by sentiment, not by logic or the absence of logic. An inability to accept this fact of life is why many managers are less than successful in their human relations.

Sentiments, of course, are feelings. We all have them, and some of the time we know they are operating. But we seldom want to admit how much they influence our actions. The fact that our feelings are formed and influenced by our age, sex, upbringing, the occasion, our personality and temperament, social status, etc. often makes us uncomfortable. We begin to realize that we don't completely control them.

Many people believe that feelings should not be allowed to affect business behavior in many situations. They prize logic, reason, and objectivity in dealing with problems. They tend to think that a person who admits his feelings in such situations is "too emotional" or "unstable." But feelings do not simply go away because they're being ignored. The result is that in many situations we try to disguise our feelings as fact or logic.

For example, suppose a manager is talking about a colleague she doesn't get along with. She is unlikely to admit her feeling openly by saying, "I just don't like the guy." Instead she says something like, "That guy is sure hard to get along with." Although this is really an expression of feeling, it sounds like an objective evaluation and is therefore more acceptable.

These two factors—the refusal to recognize that feelings exist, and the tendency to try to express them as if they were objective facts—are the source of many communication failures.

Take the opening scenario. The assistant had become worried that his boss was not satisfied with his recent performance. He couldn't say that directly, so he tried to make a case for a pay increase, hoping to get reassurance. His anxious feelings were met with logic.

Much of human communication asks for feeling, not for meaning. If superior and subordinate are to communicate effectively, the first thing the boss has to do is keep quiet and listen, trying to understand what the subordinate is really talking about, what the feelings are behind the words. Similarly, when bosses talk, they're more likely to be understood if they speak to the needs and feelings of subordinates as well as to the objectives of the company.

Having awareness of this need to listen and to understand, of course, doesn't automatically lead to practicing a true listening skill. And it is a skill. It can be developed with practice.

Listen patiently before commenting. You may be tempted to interrupt the subordinate, either because the latter is verging on unpleasantness or because you feel you understand what the subordinate is getting at. Don't do it. If there is unpleasantness, it won't go away simply because you won't permit it to be voiced. Also, you may not correctly anticipate what the subordinate is about to say.

Don't be hasty in expressing disapproval. You don't want to be seen as trying to put the employee "in his place," but rather as trying to help the person understand why he feels the way he does. One way to do this, of course, is to ask the subordinate to explain more fully what he believes to be the reasons for his feelings.

Don't argue. The big danger here is that the manager will respond to feelings with logic. The safest way to proceed is to remind yourself that the employee's feelings are not the same as yours, and that consequently it will be difficult for you to talk to these feelings.

Listen to what the person is afraid to say or cannot say without assistance. We all have trouble talking about unpleasant experiences and problems. We often need others' help (sympathy, too) to overcome the barriers. Then, too, we don't talk about some things because we regard them as so obvious that it doesn't occur to us to mention them. An example of this is racial prejudice. The person who feels strongly against a minority group seldom volunteers an explanation of why he or she feels that way, imagining that everyone can recognize the reasons.

Accept the feelings. Accept that people feel a certain emotion if they say that they do, and let them know you accept it. "I can see you feel that way." Don't try to tell them that they shouldn't feel that way. This acceptance, of course, does not mean that you necessarily share the feeling. It is merely an indication that you recognize what the other person is feeling.
   Understanding and accepting, in this sense, what the other person perceives and feels is the first step to real communication. Without acceptance, you are not communicating on the same wavelength—in effect, not communicating at all.

Find areas of agreement. Most people who are engaged in a controversial discussion will emphasize the points of disagreement. Often their awareness that they don't agree is so strong that they overlook the points on which they do agree. They lose sight of the common ground on which they might have begun a constructive discussion. Thus they set up barriers to communication when they are trying hardest to be understood.

Arguing from a point of agreement reduces antagonisms and helps to reach an accord sooner, with both parties happier and more willing to compromise. It works because you have first reached out to find what the other person thinks and believes, and have stressed the thoughts and beliefs you both have in common. This helps both of you to see the areas of disagreement more in perspective.

Letting Them Talk
There will be situations, if you have succeeded in building subordinates' trust and opened wide the communication lines, when you don't really know what to do or say. An employee comes to you with a personal problem, for example. You're not a professional counselor. But you don't want to shut the employee off.

In most cases, a manager's responsibility is to help the employee identify the problem so that he or she can begin to think about what he or she can do to solve it. Briefly, these are techniques that a manager can use in almost any personal counseling:

Create an atmosphere in which the employee feels freer to talk. Privacy is an essential ingredient, and so is freedom from time pressure.

Show understanding. Generally you'll find that all you have to do is show that you realize the employee has a problem and is going through a period of stress. You may not agree with the other person's perception of the problem or the situation. But there's no question that it exists.

Try not to judge. If it's necessary for the other person to reveal private thoughts and troubles, he or she will be more confident when you show you are not shocked by them, nor do you share them. You merely accept that they exist.

Give information as information, not advice. In the case of marital conflict, for example, you might let the employee know there are counselors and agencies (or people within your organization) available.

Countering an Attack by a Subordinate
Finally, there is the case of the employee who hurls a tirade at you. When you find yourself a target for your subordinate's angry feelings, what should you do? The answer is not instant retaliation or peremptory action. Rather, it is thoughtful appraisal.

Regard the anger as a symptom of a greater problem. The employee may not be expressing dislike of you, but rather of working conditions.

"A lot of executives," a manager once told me, "regard a blown temper in the same way as a blown fuse—something to be fixed in a hurry. You know, put another fuse in. They don't see it as a symptom, a warning to call the electrician." For this executive, the blown temper is almost always a sign of emotional overload, to be probed carefully and thoroughly.

Let the employee get it all out before you start probing for the cause. "I'm a kind of receptor," the same executive said. "I allow the person to stand or sit or pace—do whatever, except throw an ashtray. I sit there, and I try my best to be encouraging so that he will get it all out. Then I ask him to let me think over what he's said for a few hours. I suggest we get together again after lunch, or at the end of the day."

The purpose of this delaying tactic, of course, is to allow time for the subordinate to reflect, to regain composure. When the two meet again, the executive makes no reference to the flare-up, only to what caused it. "The subordinate is cooler at the second meeting," he said, "frequently apologetic. But I don't let him apologize. I say, 'Look, let's do a little analyzing.' My technique is to get his help in probing into his frustrations. And I don't penalize the guy. It seems to me that any further reference to the flare-up would be unwise."

Conduct the session behind closed doors—and keep it private. This is a matter that concerns only you and the angry subordinate, so carry on your discussion out of hearing range of other people. And don't hesitate about setting down ground rules for ensuring that what is said is not repeated later. Obviously, the employee who storms out of your office to "tell all" deserves criticism.

Even though the argument is private—even though others are not affected—there will be an emotional impact on you. You may feel extremely frustrated, even counter-aggressive, because you are really engaged in a test of emotional strength.

To maintain your cool, concentrate on getting your subordinate to find out for himself or herself what is really causing the disturbance. If the reason is legitimate, you can change the situation; if it's not, at least the person has learned something about himself or herself.

As a manager, you want to bring out the potential of your subordinates. Even in moments of anger, there are opportunities to do just that. So far as communicating is concerned, perhaps in moments of anger and strong emotions, the manager has an unparalleled opportunity to convey this message to the people who report to him or her: "What you think, feel, say is important to me. Let's never permit anything to stop you from expressing it to me."

chapter 3 Managing Performance Problems

Team-building is only one of the major challenges a manager faces, although it gets a lot of attention these days. Team maintenance is just as important a function, although one hears less about it. A manager can build a team, usually with expert assistance from professionals, in a very short time. But without continuing efforts to maintain the group's effectiveness, the team-building approach will count for very little. That effectiveness can be eroded by obsolescence, loss of confidence in one's ability, inability to recover from failure, or by a misunderstanding of the role one is to perform. The erosion of one key person's productivity can affect the entire group's.

Confronting Managerial Obsolescence

Managers suffer obsolescence, and not necessarily as a result of age or physical deterioration. More often it is a matter of immersion in routine and a gradual drift away from the mainstream.

Obsolescent managers don't see what is happening to them,

don't realize the extent of the malady until an emergency arises or a new opportunity opens up. Then they find they have inadequate resources to cope.

There are many manifestations of managerial obsolescence. Some very common ones are described below.

Taking refuge in specialty. Managers show signs of obsolescence when they respond to situations not by managing, but by going back to their specialties. The sales manager who always goes out to sell the big one, or the chief engineer who draws up the plans for every new project himself, are examples of managers taking refuge in their specialties.

Antony Jay in his book *Management and Machiavelli* calls this type of manager George I. (Even after assuming the throne of England, George I continued to preoccupy himself with the affairs of Hanover, Germany, from whence he had come). We can see George in the company president, a former sales manager who still thinks of himself as a salesman. He likes to write memos to his former colleagues in the field, encouraging correspondence from them that bypasses the new sales manager—and thus undermines him. Or take the case of the financial vice president who can't leave his controllership days behind, and who spends time wondering why the correspondence department has to have another duplicator.

Whatever an individual's special skills and experience, he or she takes on the responsibility of running an operation as a whole when that person becomes a manager. Reverting to one's specialty, doing the work of subordinates, is a step backward.

Fixing on past performance. Another sign of obsolescence is measurement of one's value to the organization by past performance or on former standards rather than by the attainment of new objectives. The manager who measures everything by past standards or achievements is settling for a more comfortable, and usually easier, routine.

Resorting to slogans. Instead of thinking problems through, the obsolescent manager resorts to slogans. "We've always done it this way" is a favorite. So is "We've tried that and it doesn't work." The frequent use of slogans like these is a good indication that it's time to consider a change in pattern, time to find ways to break out of the old routine.

Overvaluing intuition. Experience and instinct are valuable qualities, of course. But when a manager constantly skimps on factual input and "wings" decisions instead, he or she is beginning to lose touch with the real business world. Facts alone are not enough, of course, but they are necessary. A manager must be willing to seek enough information—even unwelcome information—to see things the way they really are.

There are other symptoms. Some managers successfully delegate nearly every responsibility because they are no longer able to perform confidently. Others become nuts-and-bolts administrators, elevating the importance of checking files and signing forms. Still others become devil's advocates, but their negativism is not aimed at drawing forth candid responses; it is their way to dampen others' efforts to change or to make progress.

Translate a manager's obsolescence into employee dissatisfaction, low productivity, turnover, bad decision-making, and the rest. The result is money—money drained from corporate profits. Why pay the bill? Consider these suggestions:

Match goals. How about periodically posing a very candid statement such as this to each subordinate: "This, as I see it, is where we are going; these are our goals. Now how do you see yourself fitting in?" Make them aware of the distance between the present state of the operation and where it is headed. Let them ponder both the overall requirements and the personal skills needed to reach those goals. Let them see the necessity to match their skills with those that will be needed. Most important, each subordinate should formally commit himself or herself to stated organizational goals.

Measure results. What criteria are you using to measure results? If some obsolescent managers were judged on activity alone, they'd score high, but their results—those which can be attributed to their leadership—are questionable. Management by Objectives can help. Certainly a formal appraisal system based on performance is vital.

There may be a number of reasons why obsolescent managers have ceased to grow, but one thing is indisputable: no one above them is making sure that they see the necessity to grow. No one in higher management is exercising the basic, simple, and indispensable management practice of control.

Insist on progress. Most management jobs can probably be 80 percent mastered within two years. From that point, the learning curve drops sharply. The jobholders may spend another two years learning part of the remaining 20 percent. Too often, managers who are not yet considered ready for promotion, or for whom no promotion is available, are left in the same jobs, "temporarily," of course.

The danger is that, with most of the job having become a routine, the person will fall into a rut. Even if no promotion is available, managers should be given a sense of making progress—challenging new assignments, new learning experiences, teaching opportunities, etc. It's a good idea each year, in addition to other assessments, simply to ask, "Who in my department has been in the job longer than two years?"

Encourage teamwork. To keep growing and learning, managers need to have a sense of making an essential contribution to the success of the team, where they must—and want to—pull their load. This is collaboration. Too often, however, managers are faced with what they regard as competition—a threat. They feel they are being compared with, or pitted against, other managers. Competition among managers may have some short-range benefits for a company, but it tends to encourage subterfuge, evasion, subversion of legitimate goals, etc.

Naturally, the responsibility for keeping up to date, for coping with change, for avoiding obsolescence, rests primarily on the shoulders of the subordinate. But only you, the manager, can provide encouragement—and prodding if necessary. The style you set and that set by higher management are all part of the climate. Does your organizational climate stimulate responsibility and growth? Does it stress that results are what count and what will be rewarded? Or is it a climate that encourages managers to look for hiding places, to stop growing and risking—to find ways to beat the system?

Correcting a Faulty Role Perception

To work hard used to be considered a virtue in itself. With the complexity of today's organizations, the quality and direction of work has become more important than its quantity. Today's smart managers work best by knowing where their work is taking them.

Unfortunately, the effort that employees exert in their jobs often gets considerably more attention than the direction of such effort. The result of this overemphasis on effort is often nil, because all that has actually been done is wheel-spinning. The manager engages in work that does not directly contribute to achieving desired goals and may actually achieve goals contrary to the objectives of the company or the boss.

Who bears the blame for this kind of ineffective labor? Very often the managers themselves are not quite sure what they should be doing and what ways they can best do it. Psychologists call this faulty role perception. This doesn't mean that a manager isn't working hard; on the contrary, he or she may be working much harder than is necessary. But the manager just doesn't see the job as you or top management see it. And therefore he or she, as your subordinate, will not be doing the job as you feel it should be done.

Misinterpreting the boss' view of the job. The subordinate tends to select from the boss' remarks or memos what he or she thinks is most important, and winds up with a priority which was never intended.

A classic case of this occurred two or three years ago in a plant of a large corporation's manufacturing division. Because this plant was somewhat isolated and not very large, its personnel function had been performed by the staff at a much bigger plant some distance away. But when indications of mismanagement, even dishonesty, on the part of the plant's management reached the home office, it was decided to place a young personnel manager on the scene. During his briefings at the home office, the rumors were mentioned to him, and one of the executives suggested that he should, among other things, be the eyes and ears of the home office.

Within six months the unfortunate young man was embroiled in a fierce personality and lines-of-authority conflict. He had spent too much time trying to ferret out evidence of wrongdoing instead of building a proper personnel function that would prevent possible recurrence of the rumored practices. He had exaggerated a secondary duty until it became his main objective.

Working to conform. The image of the "organization man" is pervasive and persistent. There are many aspiring managers who try to copy those further up the ladder, even to the actual styles of leadership, or to carry on essentially as their predecessors did. What such a manager doesn't consider is that the job has probably changed in its specifications. (Most jobs do over a period of time.) The manager may work very hard, but much of the energy expended will be wasted.

These are many reasons why a manager may be working hard, but not at the right things, and therefore not producing the right results. But how can they be overcome?

The very basic first step must be to define the subordinate's job with him or her. This will clarify what the real responsibilities of the job are and what you should expect from the subordinate.

The next step is to agree upon specific expected results. People change, and so do jobs. In order to assure that your subordinates are continuing to work on the same wavelength as you are, you must periodically review their jobs with them. In this way you can catch diversions of time and energy before they become dangerous.

If you are results-oriented, and your people know that they are also expected to be results-oriented, and if you and your subordinates are in agreement about what these results should be, then you will have a better chance of achieving your objectives through the people who report to you.

Stimulating the On-the-Job Retiree

Closely resembling obsolescence is retirement—on the payroll. Usually, but not always, this is an older employee.

There are several assumptions managers are quick to make when they face an older employee who seems to have retired on the job. While not always accurate, these assumptions have some validity—in some cases.

Security: The older employee is disinclined to take risks. His or her primary concern is to keep the job until pension time.

Dead end: Senior subordinates recognize that they have been passed over for advancement—promotion to management, increased income, etc. They really have no incentive to put out extra effort.

Resistance to change: Change, of course, represents a threat to the older employees' sense of security. Their self-image is at stake. Besides, why should they disturb themselves, reorient their style, take chances on failing in a new direction, when they have demonstrated mastery of the job and can continue to be successful without adopting the methods of younger people?

Reward: Older employees may have put in many hard years for the sake of their employers. They probably feel that they were not always adequately compensated during that time. Now their reduced effort is a privilege that hard work and loyalty have earned.

Any or all of these attitudes may have been adopted by the person whose performance has become increasingly disappointing. And you, as manager, can reinforce these attitudes by doing nothing about it. In which case, of course, you are helping to create a liability you can ill afford. It is not a matter of only one senior employee but your entire work force;

they will probably come to resent the extra burdens they must assume to make up for their colleague's declining performance.

That person probably represents a valuable resource; he or she possesses experience, knowledge of the operation, and seasoned judgment. Perhaps you can't stoke up the old enthusiasm, but there are ways you can help the reluctant oldster to be useful still. Some possibilities:

Expose them to new stimuli. Perhaps they can be shielded from obsolescence or premature retirement by a planned program that leads to new contacts with outside experts from other companies. It's an effort they probably will not initiate themselves. You'll have to do some prodding and planning.

One possibility is to ask the senior employee to help evaluate the seminars and workshops you are considering for training other employees. Often the programs offered by trade and professional associations, universities, etc. are difficult to assess except by a person who knows your needs. The older employee, familiar with your operation, is in an admirable position to make the evaluation—and to benefit from the outside exposure. Getting caught up in a discussion with new minds may prove an invigorating experience.

Change the scenery. Perhaps the senior person has been tied down in the home office or in one territory. Here's how one insurance executive resolved the situation. "I told my subordinate that his department was being reorganized. His new job entailed traveling to our various branch offices. Grudgingly, he agreed to the traveling. I pressed on, showing how travel could break the routine, open up new challenges, and that at times he could take his wife along quite inexpensively. Now he tells me he wonders why he was ever content to sit around in the home office in a low-pressure job."

Consider expanding responsibility. This traditional method of remotivating an employee has much in its favor. Perhaps the employee's job has become "old hat." What additional duties can you give older subordinates? How can you enlarge their responsibilities? Chances are, if they have been

conscientious, they're not going to take on additional
responsibilities and then shirk them.

Change the job completely. Maybe the senior employee
really wants a complete change. One executive describes such
a change. "My company has an orientation program for the
various departments in which employees get some insight into
what other people in the company are doing. We chose a man
who's been with the company for thirty years to conduct the
meeting. Not only does he do a whale of a job explaining the
company's operation, but he's taken a new lease on his
career." The on-the-job retiree has been transformed into an
effective inside PR man.

Assign the older employee to a task force. Task forces to
tackle certain problems or create special projects are about as
underutilized as senior subordinates on the downward side of
the performance curve. Discover new opportunities for
yourself and the experienced employee by assigning him or
her to a task force. Peer stimulation and pressure may serve to
tap resources that were no longer being exercised.
    Whatever new goals you help the older employee set,
remember to keep them:

Practical. Any re-education or change should combine the
company's needs with the individual's needs.

Specific. Each step in the process of development should
have a beginning and an end, with a time limit set for reaching
the goal.

Imaginative. Combining appeal and flexibility, so the person
doesn't get the "boxed in" or "shoved aside" feeling.

Attainable. They must be within the reach of the individual,
even though he or she may have to stretch a bit to meet them.

Aiding Recovery from a Setback
At one time or another, every manager is faced with an

employee who is psychologically distressed because of a work-related problem. It may have been a disastrous professional experience, a humiliating failure. Or it may have been something less dramatic. It could be the person whose job has been downgraded because of a merger or reorganization. It could be the sales rep who has had some important territory taken away. Or the employee to whom, through no fault of your own, you are unable to give an expected promotion.

When a person who works for you has gone through a disastrous professional experience, you can expect it to be reflected in the employee's behavior in several ways. He or she may not speak up so readily at meeings, and will play it safe, avoiding going out on a limb. When faced with an important decision, this person may defer, hedge, seek support, shy away from taking action. He or she will be highly sensitive to criticism, but without expressing it overtly, and may have the feeling that everyone is watching and waiting for another mistake.

The distressed individual finds it difficult to concentrate, to solve current problems, to be as effective as you know that person can be. Nevertheless, you depend on continued performance. The question is, do you replace him or her? If not, what can you do to help reclaim a useful resource for the organization?

Helping a once valued employee recover from a failure or work through a problem takes sensitivity and strength. It is not charity, but rather a humane and productive use of management skill. Although it can be a complicated and frustrating process, it is often preferable to replacing that person, for several reasons.

Proven performance is a known quantity. You already know what the employee can do. He or she is acquainted with the operation, and presumably is loyal.

Salvaging may be easier than replacing. The costs of advertising, traveling, interviewing, headhunter fees, training, etc. make hiring a replacement an expensive business. In addition, there is the hard-to-measure cost of disrupting the operation while the one employee leaves and the other takes over, plus the possibility that you may be forced to offer a high starting salary that plays havoc with your pay structure.

You may have a responsibility to the troubled person. The fact is, there are usually two people involved when a person's performance is substandard—the employee and the boss. This is not to say that the superior is always to blame. In fact, the question of blame is irrelevant. What is important for the manager who sees an employee slipping is to recognize that something he or she is doing, or not doing, is probably part of the employee's problem. Once a manager is able to accept the idea of implication in a subordinate's failure, it is possible to deal with the problem.

To help the employee through the period of difficulty, to help him or her back to productivity, these are some of the steps that a manager can take:

Be open about the problem. When a person is in trouble and knows it, it seems pointless for a manager to ignore it. Worse, the employee may feel the manager doesn't care. So let the distressed employee know you understand and want to help.

Don't treat the failure as a taboo subject. In your dealings with the "burned" subordinate, talk about the calamity—if there is some natural reason to refer to it, and if the reference makes a helpful point. Elaborate efforts to avoid the subject will magnify the person's feeling of being stigmatized for life.

Any such discussion should be clearly connected with improvement of the person's work now and in the future. It should focus on things and events, not on the person. "What went wrong?" is a better question than, "How did you happen to pull a boner like that?"

Discussion should be work-oriented, serious, not with a "let's laugh the whole thing off" attitude.

Emphasize past performance. This will be a reminder to both the employee's associates and to the distressed person that valued achievements are not forgotten or underrated. The effect will be to reinforce your expectation that the person will reach that level again in the near future. However, use this technique gently and sparingly. If someone is in a slump, frequent reminders of past high performance could intensify his or her depression.

Pay attention to current achievement. Calling attention to what is being done well is balm for the person in a crisis. It can help restore self-esteem and confidence. The accomplishment may not be much—only a routine job, perhaps—but it will remind the employee that you appreciate and expect good performance.

Play down present deficiencies. The troubled employee may bungle a cost estimate, a job that he or she could easily have handled in the past. But to bear down hard on the present mistake will only make it more difficult for the employee to reach his or her former capability. Therefore, don't appear to be surprised or offended by present failures. The person who has succeeded before will probably succeed again. Don't, however, completely ignore inefficiency or mistakes. A brief, matter-of-fact mention of the deficiency is far preferable to a chewing out that may convey the message, "You've done it again!" If you don't mention mistakes at all, the employee will wonder what you're really thinking.

Focus attention on what's important. Remarks like, "Is Eddie cooperating with you?" or, "Were you able to use the data I sent?" will help head the troubled person in the right direction by offering specific steps toward the completion of a task.

If possible, avoid isolation. The person in the dumps may be reluctant to leave his or her office, and not have much to say at regular meetings. But see to it that the employee attends regularly. Any "ritual" contact of this sort will help sustain a sense of solidarity with associates and thus with the job. Still, if the person is very depressed, it may be wise to arrange assignments so that they don't call for heavy face-to-face involvement with colleagues, at least for a while. Premature efforts to bring a person out of the shell may cause even more damage.

Try to build gradual progression into the employee's tasks, but don't baby. In the orientation of a new employee, there is usually a progression from easy tasks to more difficult ones. The person who is making a comeback may be experienced but have to reacquire self-assurance. To the extent that it is possible, work with this subordinate to build him or her toward the more demanding assignments and rougher confrontations. However, this doesn't mean that you should shield that employee from tough decisions or jobs. Try to lead toward them—and give unobtrusive support—but, when the difficult hurdles come, assume that the employee must face them.

Expect changes—which may be permanent. The individual who had been a brash, daring risk-taker, and who runs into disaster, may never fully reassume the old personality. After all, people do change with age, experience, and responsibility. In a person who has gone through a rough passage, that change may be considerably accelerated. Beyond a certain point, don't keep looking and hoping for the "old Harry" to come back. He may be a different person, permanently. Not a lesser person—just a different one.

When it becomes clear that this is happening, learn about, and evaluate, the new person. Harry or Harriet may be equipped for a different kind of operation, with a different future. Work with the former failure on the basis of what that person is now, not what you remember.

An important behavioral principle is that, as a manager, you are likely to get the kind of behavior from your employees that you expect to get. In the case of employees in trouble, your expectation that they will be as effective as they used to be is probably the single most important factor in pulling them through the crisis.

Working with an Excusaholic
This person's performance is erratic—sometimes excellent,

sometimes almost nonexistent. Deadlines are missed. Important projects are started and never finished. And there's always an excuse—children fell ill, the dog ran away, the car broke down, other employees let them down, they couldn't contact the necessary people, etc. Every explanation the excusaholic offers appears valid. There's always a reason for the failure. This person is one to whom things happen; he or she is accident-prone.

It's extremely difficult to censure such a person, even if you occasionally believe that illnesses are psychosomatic, that some of the accidents could have been avoided with reasonable care. It seems almost unkind to suggest that he or she experiences an unreasonable number of obstacles in performing the job.

The problem with this kind of person is that the excusaholic does not take responsibility for his or her own life. Unfortunately, this behavior pattern is not easy to change.

First, marshal your facts. Try to document each case where your expectations were not met. But don't expect ready agreement. You'll probably wind up hearing the same old reasons why the employee couldn't perform. So don't get trapped into debating how real or justified are the reasons. *They* aren't the issue. The issue is the poor performance, and that cannot continue.

At some point the employee will probably begin to abandon the excuses and start reminding you of the times when the performance was good. Agree that there were desirable, even outstanding accomplishments. You can say, "That's what makes this conversation worthwhile. When you're on top of the game, you're very good. But that doesn't happen often enough."

At this point you may suggest specific steps the person can take to improve performance—concentration on specific projects, a different pattern of working hours. Make it clear what you expect. The employee will agree sincerely, but the results may be disappointing. Just as they are unable to take responsibility for the past, excusaholics are unrealistically optimistic about the future. They don't seem to realize that they will again encounter obstacles that will provide excuses for future poor performance.

You'll have to force the person to take responsibility for certain accomplishments and goals. Make them specific and subject to a schedule. Get agreement on the level of performance you expect. Lay it on the line that good intentions are not a substitute for good performance, and that you will hold the subordinate accountable for fulfilling the promises agreed to. You may even have to say that if the goals are not achieved, there may be a salary increase withheld, a demotion, or even a termination. It's a tough stance, but it may be the only way you can shock the excusaholic into taking charge of his or her own life.

Avoiding Responsibility for Alcohol Problems

As a manager, you should ask yourself this question: Am I unwittingly helping a problem drinker to justify his or her increasing use of the bottle?

You can't, of course, take responsibility for an excessive fondness for alcohol, although that fondness can impair an employee's performance and perhaps even threaten that person's career. In the case of the person who takes longer lunches than other people, who has two or three drinks while others are having one, who is eager to join someone at a bar at the end of the day, you as manager have to make sure you don't encourage or reinforce what is going on.

Lunches. You may make it a practice to have lunch occasionally with each key subordinate. It may not be uncommon to have a drink first. But when you lunch with the heavy drinker, ask for the menu when you order the drink, and refrain from suggesting another round. The subordinate may ask for a second. But you don't have to make it easy by inviting him or her.

Or you might take the subordinate to a restaurant that does not serve booze. If you are in a place that does, suggest that you skip the drinks because you're on a tight schedule. Another option is to have lunch sent in when you want to get together with a heavy drinker. You can't stop the drinking; you just don't want to provide the excuse.

After hours. An occasional desire to have a drink before going home, especially with congenial people, is normal. But try to avoid the company of the problem drinker, if possible. What is only one occasion for you seems to the drinker to be a sanction for regular after-work boozing. "After all, the boss does it." Manage to be busy or otherwise engaged when the problem drinker invites you to join him at the bar.

Regulate the bar. At many meetings these days the booze flows freely. Sometimes the bar is open indefinitely in the hospitality suite. The program may specify that the pre-dinner bar will be open for one hour, yet liquor may continue to be available during dinner.

Shut the bar down when you planned to. Light and moderate drinkers won't care that much. Generally the only ones who will care are those who don't need the extra booze.

If you have a policy that bar bills at meetings are to be picked up by the people who incur them, stick to that rule. Often such a policy is stated, but disregarded in practice. Once again, the heavy drinker is the one who benefits by not having to pay.

One especially delicate problem is what to do with the valued employee who takes frequent long lunches and comes back half smashed. If you ignore it, you are likely to convey signals of approval or at least tolerance to the problem drinker. You might consider saying instead, "Look, Sam, you're showing the effects of your lunch. If you're not smashed, people think you are. I'd like to give you a choice: Take the afternoon off and go home, or let me shut your door so you can get some rest."

You probably won't stop the drinking. But you will signal loud and clear how you feel about it. The subordinate will at least know you are not winking at his behavior. He or she may feel it necessary to confine the heavy drinking to nonworking hours. If you have to take stern action, such as requiring the problem drinker to seek help, you will have paved the way by avoiding encouragement of the practice and signaling disapproval of those acts that interfere with performance.

✿ ✿ ✿ ✿ ✿ ✿ ✿

Whatever the nature of the threat to the work group—the employee who is performing poorly or who is working counter to your and the organizational objectives—there is no way you can avoid taking necessary and corrective action. Not only is the person producing disproportionately, but perhaps even more serious is the effect of one person's slacking off on other employees who report to you. At first others in the department may extend a fair amount of tolerance to the unproductive person. But if the problem isn't confronted and corrected, that tolerance turns to bewilderment, and finally to outright resentment. If the problem person is a manager, that manager's employees will be looking for better leadership.

A single problem person, through his or her effect on everyone else in the work group, becomes an outrageously expensive liability for the manager who cannot or does not deal effectively with that person.

chapter 4 Dealing with Challenges to Your Leadership

✗ Some behavior problems constitute an indirect threat to
effectiveness—yours and your employees'. They may not
immediately involve productivity. Rather, their initial impact
may be on morale, communication, an employee's perception
of self or relationships with others. But if these challenges to
your leadership are not dealt with, they could go beyond
being irritating and become seriously disruptive.

Reinforcing the Wrong Image.
Managers are often lured into encouraging incompetent
behavior, or at least an employee's image of him- or herself as
ineffectual. Here's how one secretary was reinforced in her
feeling that she was incompetent, "not OK" in Transactional
Analysis terms.

BOSS: This letter is very important. It's going to a major
        customer and it has to be letter-perfect.
SECTY: Oh, Pauline, I don't think you ought to give that
        to me. You know how many mistakes I make
        when I type letters.

BOSS: Hmm. Perhaps you're right. I'll ask Susan to do
          it.

This secretary has been playing a game that can be labeled
Kick Me. Everyone plays games from time to time. In this
case, her game has succeeded.

However, if the boss were to assume the Adult ego state (as
defined by Transactional Analysis), the scenario might go like
this:

BOSS: Are you saying you really see yourself as
          incompetent?
SECTY: I think so.
BOSS: I'm very sorry about that. Why do you think this
          way? Can you give me some examples?
SECTY: I never get things right.
BOSS: *Sometimes* that happens. It does to all of us. So,
          we ought to be thinking about what specific
          things we can do to help you turn out better
          work.

This type of response can be helpful to any manager faced
with an employee who insists upon being regarded as unable
to do things right. Some guidelines:

Don't rush to agree. That's only confirming the employee's
view. Ask questions to get more information.

Insist on specifics. Don't let the other person take refuge in a
generality. Specifically, how does he or she justify these
negative feelings?

Play down the uniqueness. The characteristic he or she thinks
is unique is shared by most people at times. Everyone does
dumb things now and then.

Require a plan for improvement. Get the other person to
dwell less on the existence of the problem and more on a plan
for eliminating it. Be very positive and firm about insisting on

improvement. That way you won't reinforce behavior that in the long run can't do either of you any good.

Toning Down the Temperamental Wunderkind

At the other extreme you may have the genuinely gifted subordinate whose perception of self causes great problems. This person is often temperamental, easily irritated, constantly ranting about the obstacles put in his or her path or the lack of cooperation. For you this means time (and sometimes self-respect) lost in coddling and cajoling. Like other bosses of "mad geniuses," you may see only three alternatives in dealing with this person.

Status quo at any cost. You could reach for a tranquilizer and start trying to calm down your brilliant subordinate. That way, you would lessen the risk of alienating this indubitably valuable employee.

Limited reproof. You could tell the wunderkind to stop carrying on over something that can't be helped and behave as any other employee would in the circumstances. However, this employee is probably aware of his worth to the company, and also knows he or she is not like "any other employee." So there probably won't be much impact with this approach.

Laying it on the line. "I've had all of this I'm going to take," you could shout back. "Either you change your ways and start acting like a reasonable person or you're through." The subordinate might be so used to giving free rein to his own temperament that he would lose control and jump to a conclusion no one truly wants.

Many an organization wins success through the ideas of a single gifted individual. Yet when talent is combined with a disruptive temperament, the organization is continually beset by emotional outbreaks that damage efficiency and morale. Other employees resent the special handling that the *enfant terrible* receives. For you it may be like living on the edge of a volcano.

If you have a "mad genius" on your staff, take the time to

ponder a crucial question. Is the employee really worth the trouble? There are two factors to consider here:

Cost. What will it cost in profits if this particular person leaves? If the cost is going to be high, then top management will probably think it worth just about any price to keep the especially gifted employee. Some organizations provide lavish quarters, special hours and working conditions, and generous budgets to keep their resident supertalent happy. (A rival company might do the same, if he or she could be lured away.)

There is, however, an implicit bargain struck when management accedes to such arrangements. The genius is expected to produce, and to keep producing. You may have to keep records of productivity. Often managers let past accomplishments color their views of how the talented subordinate is currently performing.

Other people. In most cases, the special treatment of any one individual is resented by the group in which he or she works. If the people in your department feel such resentment, it may help if you commiserate with them, using a touch of humor and pointing out that you're in the same boat, but you all have to recognize that geniuses are different. If, however, the favored-child situation leads to reduced departmental efficiency and/or high turnover, you should let your superiors know that this is another price the company is paying for its permissive attitude.

If you decide your subordinate really is indispensable, it might be best to change your attitude toward him or her. Learn to tell yourself when a scene begins, "This too will pass." Refuse to argue. Let each storm take its course. And try to put these tempests-in-a-teapot into perspective in your own life. Keep your self-respect by keeping your sense of humor and let him or her know you can't be "bugged" no matter what.

Looking Beyond the Continual Complaints
The subordinate who is never satisfied about vacation policy,

fringe benefits, work assignments, etc. can be a burden on your time and nerves. Continual challenges to every decision can drive even the most tolerant executive to the point of explosion.

Look behind the surface of the gripe, however, and you may find that what the person is really saying is one or more of the following:

Recognize me. The complainer may not really expect you to solve the problems presented. Instead, what's wanted is recognition of the trials he or she must undergo to get the job done. To this person, all that's really needed is a statement such as, "I understand your concern. One thing I admire is that you keep doing a fine job, whatever the obstacles."

Please don't criticize me. Even proven performers may feel insecure about their abilities, especially when confronted with a novel assignment or task. The complaining may be a way of justifying in advance the failure they fear. What they want is reassurance that you're not interested in catching them in mistakes. You can reassure them by avoiding advice that might be taken as criticism. Instead, ask questions about what can be done to solve the problem.

See that I'm upset. In handling gripes, it's important to remember that the complainer's feelings may be more important than the complaint itself. If you fail to deal with those feelings, the person may keep returning with the same grievance, perhaps under different guises.

When you see that an employee is angry or upset about a problem, acknowledge the feeling. "You're angry because you think the expediter nearly fouled up your schedule." Or, "You're really annoyed about making that miscalculation." Sometimes subordinates may not be looking for anything more from you than the realization that they are downright unhappy about a problem—and not unreasonably so.

Even with chronic complainers, it's good to keep in mind that this time around, the grievance may be justified. Just because you've heard it before—"that jerk in statistical services really fouls us up"—doesn't mean it isn't true this time. Or perhaps this particular person is the only one with the courage to tell you, "Our wage and salary policy is lousy." Maybe it is. Listening, coupled with solution-oriented questions about the problem, makes sure that you don't make false assumptions about the validity, or lack of validity, of complaints.

Dealing with Defensiveness

But, then, there are times *you* want to complain to a subordinate, to criticize his performance. The problem is that the employee does not take kindly to being criticized. Or he or she is going through a difficult time and so is especially sensitive to criticism about work.

Dealing with a thick-skinned colleague can drive even the most placid manager to the aspirin bottle. It is natural to feel some resentment toward a person who seems to find a slight where none is intended. You tell yourself there must be ways to reduce the likelihood of offending a person who is easily miffed.

There are. Before you consider them, however, fix it in your mind that thin skin is a problem for the people who have it, not for you. In fact, if you take it too seriously you may find the condition is catching. So it's in your own interest not to get too involved while making reasonable efforts to ease the suffering. Here are some methods to try:

Get right to the point. It's tempting to open up a performance counseling session with idle pleasantries. The subordinate, however, is probably expecting you to get to the problem. Consequently, any delay will only increase anxiety about what you have to say.

Keep your remarks brief. The longer you talk, the greater the chance that you'll repeat yourself, and the greater the possibility that the deficiency you're talking about will be blown out of proportion in the other person's mind.

State the problem factually. Start by describing specific evidence of a problem. "Absenteeism in your department has risen almost 20% in the last three months." Don't ask why or demand to know what the subordinate is going to do about it. Rather, sit back for a few moments and wait for a response to your statement.

Challenge the employee. When you suspect you're not getting through, you may be tempted to say, "If you weren't so bull-headed, you'd listen to me and follow my advice." Say instead, "Look, all I'm asking you to do is try. It may get the thing out Wednesday or it may not, but there's only one way to find out. Give it a try."

Recognize some of the behaviors that hurt—and some that help: For example, what comes across to you as gentle kidding may be translated by a sensitive colleague as a dig or sarcasm. This certainly won't help. Also, a little criticism goes a long way with this type of person. Don't fire salvos about the behavior that you are criticizing. Instead, you might raise questions. Ask if the person sees something you don't in the circumstances surrounding the behavior; ask if you fully understand.

Avoid arguing with the explanation given. The employee's immediate reaction is likely to be self-justification. If you argue or try to make suggestions at this point, you may only provoke further self-justification. Instead, echo the explanations in simple declarative form. This will encourage your subordinate to get to the real root of the problem—which you, after all, may not be aware of. For example, "You feel the standards are unrealistic." This should keep the discussion moving.

It may also be necessary to encourage the employee's analysis of the problems by asking occasional questions. But remember, "How" questions tend to foster cooperation, while "Why" questions generally tend to foster defensiveness. So ask, "How can we solve it?," not "Why did it happen?" Ask if the person sees something in the circumstances surrounding the behavior that you don't see; ask if you fully understand. Always make sure you are both tuned in to the same channel. "I see, Bob, what you are saying is . . . ."

Accept the person's feelings. If the person becomes hurt or defensive, recognize how he or she feels, and acknowledge it. "John, no one likes criticism of his work. I know how you feel. I'm not interested in putting you down. But my job is to see that everyone here works at optimum level, and I'm not doing my job when I overlook work that isn't at that level."

Recognizing how a person feels, however, does not mean that you should reinforce the feeling. On the contrary, apologizing, commiserating, or sympathizing will just dig the person in deeper. Rather, you simply—and briefly—let John know that you recognize his hurt feelings.

Remember that suggestions go further than disparaging comments. Instead of saying, "Barbara, that won't work," say, "What would happen if we...." That helps to keep the person's mind on the situation, not on the emotions aroused by any remark which can be interpreted as a slam.

Be as positive as possible. Help the sensitive person to see what needs to be done, rather than what he or she failed to do. Don't say, "The reason you didn't see my memo is that you're not organized." Rather, "Perhaps you might find it helpful to do what I do, which is to check my in box each day."

Stress the rewards that can come from correcting performance. Say something like, "You may feel that Bill dislikes you, but if you could just work with him on this project, we could get it out by Wednesday instead of Friday. That would give you two more days to get a start on that project you've been wanting to tackle." This is eminently more effective than saying, "You know, I think you and Bill ought to try to get along better with each other."

It helps the employee to realize that it is in his own best interest for the two of them to function together.

Once you've arrived at a solution, sum up the situation yourself or have the employee do so. That way there will be no misunderstanding about what has to be done. It is also a good idea to make arrangements for a follow-up meeting or at least to check back later to make sure no further problems have been encountered and that progress is being made.

Finally, recognize that sincere and deserved praise is particularly important to someone who is overly sensitive. When the person has done something praiseworthy, say so and spread the word to others.

Feeling Sensitive about Humor

Occasionally you may find yourself the butt of an employee's humor. You are having the tail pinned on you. Although, as a manager, you can afford to go along with humor at your expense up to a point, there are several basic considerations you should be aware of.

The nature of relationships that depend on constant joking is discussed in greater detail in Chapter Five, "De-fanging the Joking." Although the emphasis there is on joking relationships among colleagues, many of the same characteristics apply in a manager-subordinate situation. The joking is basically unfriendly, an indication of anger or hostility.

You may have someone on your hands who harbors a grievance against you. Humor can also be a form of criticism. You may believe that things are running well in your department, since you've had no feedback from employees to convince you otherwise. However, the needling may be an indication that all is not well in the operation. A third possibility is that the needler wants your job, and uses belittling humor to cut you down.

A manager who puts up with continued joking at his or her expense is tolerating a destructive situation, demeaning to the manager and embarrassing to other employees.

Methods for dealing with such humor are also discussed in greater detail in Chapter Five. The manager must treat the joke seriously, resist the temptation to reply in kind, and try to get to the bottom of the other person's resentment.

Sound the humorist out. You might say something like, "You've got a pretty keen eye for what goes on here. But sometimes when I laugh at what you say, I get the feeling that maybe you're trying to tell me something I ought to be taking seriously." Keep your approach good-humored. This may persuade the critic that he or she is doing too much of a good thing and to exercise some self-censorship.

Consider telling the humorist how you feel. Most of us don't really know the full impact we have on others, so it's possible the joker doesn't know how the needling affects you. If you can convey that the clowning is hurting your relationship, you may find the employee willing to tone it down. The danger, however, is that he may get even more pleasure out of the jokes at your expense.

Don't pull rank. Getting stuffy just gives the needler a bigger and better target for the barbs.

Take the departmental temperature. It could be time for you to talk to others in the department, to discover any hidden problems. Do your best to create an atmosphere in which people feel free to talk—and keep your eyes and ears open.

Most important, bear in mind that, even if you persuade yourself that what the clown says leaves you unscathed, you probably won't convince anyone else.

Fending Off Others' Work

Your sales training manager asks your help in selecting the site for the next training meeting; a production supervisor wants you to help him arbitrate a feud between two of his people; a branch manager asks you to help decide which of two equally qualified men to hire.

Is your response similar to any of the following ones?

"I'll get back to you on this."

"Leave this with me and I'll go over it."

"Let me think about it."

When this sort of thing happens, a transaction takes place.

The subordinate transfers a problem, and the manager gets an additional headache. The practice is insidious. Sometimes it seems like the easiest way to take care of the immediate situation, but in the long run, it will only cause problems in the future. Taking problems out of the hands of subordinates does not help their growth, and it can diminish your effectiveness. The manager who makes too many of these transactions will find less and less time and energy available for managerial tasks.

Another possible consequence is that the manager may forget about the problem he or she has implicitly assumed responsibility for. When this happens, nothing gets done, and subordinates begin to think of the boss as someone who doesn't follow through.

How can you stay out of situations like this?

The answer lies in the wording of the response you must make when it becomes apparent that a subordinate is trying to escape the burden of a problem. The best response is not, "What can we do to solve this problem?" It is, rather, "When this conversation ends, which of us is going to carry the burden of worrying about this thing?"

Define the responsibility. You may want to say something like, "Okay, Jim, in the next half hour or so let's see what we can do about this problem. Maybe we can solve it. At least we can both see it more clearly. But let's understand each other— when we're finished talking about it, I'm going to expect you to come up with the final answer."

Set a timetable. "Have we thrashed out all the questions? I guess we haven't yet got the answer, but we're closer to it, don't you think? Now, how about getting back to me on progress? Would a week from tomorrow be time enough for you?"

Forget it. Even when you've handled the situation adroitly during the interview, there may still be a lingering anxiety—"I wonder if he's really clear on how to handle it," or a vague feeling of guilt—"Maybe I could have pitched in a little more on the thing." Since the whole idea of the procedure is that the subordinate has to come up with the answer, the logical next step for you is to forget about it, temporarily. You've made a note of when Jim is due to come back and report. The mental decks should now be cleared so that you can turn your full attention to your own problems.

Integrating the Employee with a Past

No one could seriously question your need to know as much about the on-the-job behavior of your key people as possible. But how much weight should you give to information about an employee that you get from another manager? Or to rumors about a new employee?

One manager faced this problem when a bright young engineer was transferred to his division. The manager had heard from a colleague that the engineer was heavily and publicly critical of the way things were done in his department. With this in mind, the manager made a point of saying during orientation, "I believe in being on the level with the guys I work with, right from the start. It's probably no surprise to you that I've heard you can do a lot of griping in public when things aren't run the way you think they ought to be. I just wanted you to know that I don't go for that in my operation. I mean, if you've got something on your mind, you spill it to me—nobody else. Do you read me?"

The new engineer nodded.

"Good," the manager replied. Smiling now, he got up and shook the engineer's hand. "Glad to have you with us."

The discussion broke up with seeming candor and cordiality. But it was only an appearance. The manager had angered his new subordinate, had seriously undermined the chances for trust and a productive working relationship between them, because the engineer's negative attitude to the employer was only hearsay.

When you accept a new employee, regardless of the negative or critical things you or other employees may have heard about him or her, keep these pointers in mind.

Evaluate current performance. If you haven't had a chance to see any performance yet, reserve your judgment until you have. That means, of course, forgetting for the moment the things you have heard.

Don't reinforce the behavior you don't want. An employee who has had a bad relationship with a previous boss may bring a lingering distrust of anyone in authority. When that person sees signs of suspicion, criticism, etc. on your part, he or she may feel, "It's going to be more of the same. No matter what I do, I'll be wrong. So why bother?"

In the case of the young engineer, the lack of trust between his boss and him certainly won't encourage him to take his complaints to the boss. Chances are he'll voice his complaints to his colleagues. Ironically, the manager has reinforced the very behavior he doesn't want.

Be positive about the behavior you've been warned about. Suppose the manager had said this to the new employee. "I get the impression that you're a pretty candid, imaginative person, and I'm looking forward to benefiting from your ideas. So anytime you want to suggest some changes, don't hold back; I want to hear from you." Certainly the reaction would have been a great deal more positive than the one that actually occurred.

As a manager your aim undoubtedly is to produce a climate that encourages the best behavior and performance that the employee is capable of. Even so, after your openness, your patience, your positive direction, the new person may still prove to be what you were told he or she is. But then at least you have the consolation of knowing that the failure to change was, in fact, the other person's, not yours.

Most of the above recommendations can be applied as easily to a new person whose reported past is one of outstanding achievement. Pluses can be as easily exaggerated as minuses, and a new manager's uncritical acceptance of glowing reports can be just as hazardous as believing the worst.

Deciding What to Do about the Office Affair

What do you do about those employees who are creating their "past" right now—say, by having an affair?

Of course, people's attitudes toward sex seem to be changing radically. The couple having an affair may be right in anticipating less criticism than they would once have provoked. Still, you can safely assume that there will be gossip about the lovers, some expression of disapproval, and attempts to find out how you feel about the romance and what, if anything, you plan to do about it.

There is a lot of talk these days about how managers should consider the "whole person" when dealing with employees. As a recognition that employees have personal goals and needs that influence their performance, it makes managerial sense. Yet that is not to say that a manager should probe into another person's private life. In fact, such interference can easily give subordinates the impression their boss thinks he or she owns them.

If you feel you should try to stop an affair, you ought to consider possible consequences. For example, you could alienate people who are not involved, but who would view your efforts as repressive and suspect that you might someday try to judge their morals, too. You could leave yourself and the company open to legal action if you try to pin the blame on one of the lovers. One woman who was fired because of an affair successfully sued her former company, charging she had been discriminated against since, as frequently happens, the man involved kept his job.

If you use the romance as an occasion to demonstrate your tolerance, you run other risks. You can alienate the people who do not approve, and you can also become more involved than you want to be, if the couple start seeking you out for advice.

The best course of action is usually to ignore the whole thing, unless the couple's work performance is continually affected, or unless there is concrete evidence that official confidences have been breached or co-workers object so strongly that departmental morale plummets.

If the liaison offends your personal code, if you worry about the families affected by the affair, such a see-no-evil, speak-no-evil, hear-no-evil policy will not be easy for you. Still, you may find that it is the wisest course.

If co-workers object to your refusal to step in, you should remind them you cannot in fairness act on the basis of what may or may not be going on. You might, however, find it wise to caution the couple that their behavior is causing talk, whether justified or unjustified. It's up to them, then, to behave with the discretion commonly expected of reasonable adults.

In some cases managerial skill can be applied more successfully to the reactions of co-workers than to the lovers or alleged lovers. An illustration of this was provided by a department head in a midwest insurance company. One of his employees passed on to the manager a rumor that two of the female clerical employees were involved in a homosexual affair.

The department head thanked the employee noncommittally for his information. In the following days, he quietly observed the two subjects of the rumor. He noticed that the women were discreet, that their performance had not fallen. He concluded that the biggest difficulty in this situation was with their colleagues who, hearing the rumor, reacted either in disgust or in ridicule.

The manager called the rumor-spreaders, one by one, into his office. "What we're concerned with in this department is quality and quantity of performance," he said to each. "What people do or say off the job doesn't interest me. But on the job—that's my business, and I'm going to deal with any word or act that interferes with performance." The rumors stopped. His people, aware of the manager's tough attitude, were forced to conceal their antipathy toward the alleged lesbians and work with them cooperatively.

When the situation is one where work suffers and warnings about performance have no effect, then you may have no choice but to transfer or fire the individuals. If so, you must keep in mind the laws against discrimination. What is sauce for the goose is sauce for the gander these days; and to avoid legal complications, both people involved in the affair must be treated the same.

An extramarital office romance stimulates the prurient interest of some people and arouses moral objections in others. If you can ride out the initial reactions, you'll often find that, in response to the notoriety, the couple themselves will moderate their behavior and get on with the work.

Handling an Employee's Personal Problem

Sometimes a subordinate has a personal problem, one which he or she can't seem to leave at the door to the office or plant. There is illness in the family. Perhaps a spouse is threatening to leave. A child is experimenting with drugs.

It's the kind of personal difficulty you don't want to get involved in. You're a manager, not a father, moral critic, or psychoanalyst. Yet you are concerned when you see the employee's morale and confidence dipping, performance lagging, and relations with you, co-workers, and subordinates deteriorating as a consequence of the crisis. So you are stuck with the problem, even though you don't want it. Some considerations:

Don't let the person bottle up the problem. The tendency of many of us is to try to keep up a brave front when trouble strikes. This creates an extra tension, the tension of having to act normally. It makes it impossible for the employee to get the support that co-workers can provide. Striving to smile at all the right times, he or she may become obsessed with worrying. "Do they know? Have I given myself away?"

Encourage the employee in trouble to let his or her feelings be known around the department, or at least to acknowledge that he or she is confronted with a problem. The mere admission of the existence of a problem, psychologists point out, removes the burden of dissembling.

Should the manager go further? There are certain kinds of problems—illness, impending death, finances—where the mere fact of listening can give the employee support and understanding.

For some kinds of problems, however, listening may not be a good idea. The wise manager parries an employee's attempts—in a marital crisis, for example—to go into intimate details. For what psychologists call "negative transference" may set in; the employee may come to resent the manager who knows so much, forgetting that the manager had not encouraged the employee to reveal the problem.

Use work, or rest from it, as an antidote. Essentially there are two reactions to personal problems in relation to work. Some people seek to bury their emotions in frenzied work. Others are too emotionally disoriented to work with their usual effectiveness. For those who can escape into their work, you can provide work. You can load them up, to use the words of one manager. For others, you provide time off or a temporary reassignment of some of their responsibilities. A long-term acquaintance with the employees may give a clue as to which type they are. Otherwise, it's a matter of testing; load up, or ease up, and observe the reaction.

What you decide to do in any given situation must, of course, depend on several factors—the person, the nature of the problem, your relationship with the individual, etc. You have to determine whether you can credibly offer counsel or suggest professional help elsewhere. Or whether you should do anything but listen and express concern. But a strict "hands off" policy is seldom satisfactory where a valued subordinate is involved. Not only may it damage organizational effectiveness, but in effect it denies the subordinate recognition as a person—a whole person.

chapter 5 Getting Results Across Lines

Most managers share responsibility with those in other departments not under their authority. Few managers can achieve the results they aim for without the active cooperation of others. Getting an insurance policy issued, marketing a piece of equipment, filling an airplane with passengers and getting it to fly—all require the cooperation of people whose management, departmental climates, criteria for performance, levels of morale and job satisfaction, and personalities are different.

The vice president of marketing may know what is necessary to promote, distribute, and merchandise a product. But for profitable pricing the expertise of the financial people is needed. For quality and delivery the marketing executive needs the support of purchasing, engineering, and production. Without personnel there would be no one to sell and service the product. And so on. At each level the same need for interdepartmental support and cooperation exists, although perhaps to a lesser degree at lower levels.

Solving Interdepartmental Problems
In a bureaucracy—which is what most organizations are—

crossing functional boundaries usually requires tact, diplo-
macy, and maybe even a lot of gritting of the teeth. People's
functions are fairly well set—you do this, she does that, he
does something else. You have little room for changing things
around.

On an organizational chart the functions are shown in the
little black boxes. Who runs what is also sharply indicated by
the lines that run up and down to connect the boxes. When one
manager can't get the results desired from a manager in a
different box, the first manager might plead, cajole, even
threaten a punch in the nose. It might work; it might not. For
chances are the other manager is in a different line of
authority. Unless a manager works in an unusually enlightened bureaucracy, therefore, he or she has to show skill,
patience, and a willingness to take risks to achieve strong
cooperative ties with peers.

For example, a bank officer whose jurisdiction includes
customer relations noted a significant increase in complaints
of inaccuracies in the records of new customers that seemed
attributable to computer errors. So she suggested that
members of her staff hold a meeting with representatives of
the operations department to talk about the increased
customer complaints. But the meeting was a dismal failure.
Her assistant described his reaction. "They were all over the
place, even criticizing the quality of the customer contact
people who are being hired. I just couldn't see how that kind
of thing helps, and I told them so."

The chief representative of the operations group had a
different interpretation. "They kept saying that we should
leave no stone unturned, anything we wanted to mention that
could help the situation, fine. So we brought up a couple of
ideas, and they started getting defensive as hell. I don't think
we accomplished anything but raise more dust."

What happened was that, after she outlined the major
problems and complaints, the customer relations manager
said, "I'm open to any suggestions." She said it two or three
times. The other group accepted the invitation at face value—
and ran into a hornet's nest.

There were at least two major problems. The first had to do
with the high turnover of people who sat behind the desks in

lobbies of branch banks. They were not well paid, and tended
to leave when their dissatisfaction reached intolerable levels.
The other problem was caused in part by the proliferation of
checking and savings plans brought about by competitive
pressures. The variety of forms used introduced more
opportunities for errors, especially among new reps. The
operations people suggested more careful training. But when
they suggested this solution, the customer relations manager
became angry and complained that the discussion was going
off on a tangent.

Actually, she had been sincere in saying she wanted an open
discussion. She had determined to her satisfaction where the
fault lay—in the operations department itself. She was sure
that, when all the facts were put on the table, the other side
would come to the same conclusion.

It's quite human to assume that other departments will see
the problem your way, especially when you present all of the
"facts." Life doesn't work that way, however, and the
tendency to make such an assumption is only one of the
pitfalls facing a manager who wants to work across departmental lines. In your own efforts to improve collaboration
with other managers, consider these suggestions.

Let them define the problem as they see it. The odds are that
you don't know all the factors in the situation, even if you
think you do. It is most important to allow others to describe
the problem from their viewpoints and to explore why
viewpoints diverge. You'll often find that individuals differ
widely in their conceptions of what a particular department's
or individual's responsibility is. Unless these differences are
understood and admitted, the group can never speak a
common language.

One way many managers avoid accusatory definitions such
as, "What you've been doing that fouls us up is . . ." is to first
define the solution that everyone would like to see exist. In the
bank's problem, the number of inaccuracies should be no
more than x percent.

Be as open as possible. In almost any prolonged communication between departments, there will be some sensitive or

confidential area touched upon. Such secrets can be liabilities. There is no easy way to handle an encroachment. Honesty is the best guideline. If you've been asked not to reveal certain information, say so. "I'm sorry, but this is an area I've been asked not to go into." Or, "Could we postpone this until I can check with the boss?" If the authority to tell or not to tell is yours, consider which will pose the greater problem, revealing the confidential information or withholding it. People in other departments may be especially quick to resent what seems to be an attempt to hold back. Withholding information may appear as a lack of trust. If you can't steer the discussion away from confidential areas, then at least try to explain why you can't divulge all your information.

Keep your eye on the objective—a solution. In any inter-departmental dialogue, some suggestions or solutions will not be entirely to your liking, especially if they seem to imply criticism. But don't yield to the urge to jump in and defend yourself against alternative answers which you may already have decided are unsuitable. Chances are, the other managers are just as anxious to get to the truth as you are, and not at all as eager to embarrass you as you might be tempted to think. Sit back and let the suggested solutions be presented, examined, discussed. Your lack of defensiveness will encourage more objective evaluation from others. By the same token, it is important to offer your own suggestions as inoffensively as possible. Asking, rather than telling, is often the best way to do this. "What's your reaction to this—suppose we were to . . ."

Take sufficient time. Too many managers enter an inter-departmental conference with the assumption that everything can be cleared up in one session. They become frustrated when seemingly extraneous matters are brought up, and the problem seems to move away from solution rather than toward it. But the problem may have an extensive root system. When different perspectives are brought to bear, it is likely to grow rather than diminish.

A first meeting can be rated extremely successful if the participants can agree on what the critical issues are and what should be explored further. After all, if the solution were really simple and obvious, it probably wouldn't be necessary to have the meeting in the first place. And, continuing the plant analogy, too fast action may result in pulling up just the top of the weed, leaving the roots to flourish.

It's very difficult, before a conference with other managers, to try to think through the situation as you believe the other people see it. Their behavior at the meeting may puzzle and annoy you. But after all, they have a rationale for behaving as they do, even if you don't see it. And they probably feel as rational and justified as you do.

Being a Graceful Winner

Negotiation is a key word in describing what happens—or should happen—when two or more departments try to resolve their common difficulties. Unfortunately there are managers who try to force everyone to take sides and turn the dealings into a situation where one side wins, one loses. Actually, winning all the points is not a good idea, because the forced agreement will not sit easy. The subsequent resentment is enough to jeopardize the agreement. The party who has been forced to knuckle under will probably work in every way to get the decision reversed, or to find some sort of revenge. Remember, even after you have won your fight, you have to keep working with those people. The way they feel about you and about what you have done can have a profound impact on your continuing effectiveness. Even those who sided with you may cause problems. They may ask that you reciprocate their support later, when it is not in your interest to do so, or they may expect you to show gratitude for their support by favors or special treatment.

At one time or another, nearly everyone risks ignoring the human factor in his or her battles. Impatient managers are often sorely tempted to drop a blockbuster or two when it may not be necessary. If you find yourself facing such a temptation, you might do well to consider these cautionary points.

Determine how evenly you and the other people are matched. This can help you determine the degree of strength you'll need to get what you want. Never use more force than you have to. When you display too much power, people become anxious and disinclined to work closely with you. They'll be wary about trying to resolve mutual problems with you.

Decide ahead of time what you can afford to give up. Even if total victory seems realistically possible, and even if the facts seem to be all on your side, it's better to find something you can afford to concede to the "loser." Again, you have to keep working with these people.

Stop when you've won your goal. Don't use a victory as an immediate stepping-stone to other requests, other demands. Some managers say to themselves, "Well, as long as we're hot, we might as well go for some of those things we've been wanting for a long time." You will have more strength later if you stop now, satisfied with what you've achieved. People will be more willing to talk with you in the future about mutual problems if they don't fear a massacre.

Take the initiative in healing the wounds. Grace in victory is even more rare than grace in defeat. It should be as highly respected. Indicate by your attitude that you are not smug or gloating about your triumph, and make specific moves of reconciliation to your opponent. Offer your cooperation, and whatever other resources you have, to make another's defeat easier to swallow.

Although you may not, in fact, look upon your campaign as a win-lose situation, others probably do. No one likes to be a loser. The more you can do to give the other people a feeling they have won something, too, the better your chances of getting along with them in the future.

De-fanging the Joking
It isn't fair, even in the most rigid bureaucracies, to say that little or no horizontal communication exists between departments—although one sometimes hears this. There is always some kind of information flow. In some situations

there is a habitual resort to humor, so that joking relationships exist between people and departments.

Anthropologists have found that among certain peoples—the Crow Indians, for one—joking relationships are prevalent. One person or one group of people habitually makes fun of another, who is not allowed to take offense. Behind their conduct, it is believed, lies a fear of the conflict that threatens to erupt if the joking relationship should cease.

Something of the sort can be found among executives. I'm not talking about the kind of banter used to pass the time among friends, or the humor that often arises spontaneously when a work team has to get through a crisis. The classic joking relationship is something quite different. Basically, it is unfriendly. The unacknowledged intention of those who indulge in it is to sidestep a conflict that seems too hot to handle.

At a seminar I observed four managers from the same corporation who all had a working relationship with one another. Watching them together, one would assume that they had a marvelously secure relationship. During breaks and in the evenings they clustered. Their conversations were studded with jokes on and funny jibes at each other, especially toward one of the four whose name was Bill. But toward the end of the seminar, conflict erupted. One of the four accused Bill of always trying to dominate whatever group he was in. Then the fragile knot came untied. They were not at all secure in their relationship. They were in fact hostile and afraid, especially of Bill. Their constant joking covered up an unpleasant reality.

A group that insists upon joking relationships is much less cohesive than it appears superficially. Unlike people who use humor or wit for its own sake, the constant jokers are often doing demonstrable damage in the following ways:

Issues remain unresolved among them. Many conflicts should not be shoved out of sight. Hinting at them indirectly, trying to laugh them away, leaves the underlying problem unresolved. It is not even recognized.

Criticism is too well camouflaged. Employing jokes to

camouflage criticism almost inevitably leads to underplaying the seriousness and the full dimensions of the problem under review. A lot of vital, helpful information can get lost this way.

Effort is wasted. If nothing can be said until a humorous wrapping for it can be found, meetings and even simple conversations become elaborate and time-consuming. No one feels free to state opinions and criticisms directly and clearly.

Responsibility becomes hard to assign. Too much horseplay confuses the specifics of what should be done by whom. The game takes on more importance in the players' eyes than their work.

If you find yourself part of a group that constantly relies on joking relationships, what can you do to put a stop to it?

Take the game seriously. You don't have to be a sourpuss, but don't participate. Don't laugh or retaliate in kind. At times you'll be tempted to join in the fun—when it seems harmless, or when you feel a little embarrassed to sit there with a straight face. Keep in mind, however, that if you do go along, you are encouraging what is basically a vicious game.

Insist on explanations. When messages are consistently presented as humor, ask people to clarify them for you. Make sure instructions are repeated straight—who does what when? It may be uncomfortable to appear not to understand the private jokes, but this is probably your best technique for forcing the jokers to communicate—at least with you—in a different way.

Intercede when necessary. If another person, subordinate or colleague, seems to be everybody's dunce, stop the game. The simplest way to break it off is by changing the subject. However, be prepared for a curious phenomenon. The scapegoat may accept the role and be quite reluctant to have you intercede. It unmasks the game, for one thing. For another, it forces both aggressors and victim to confront real issues.

Bring the conflict to the surface eventually. After you've been with the group long enough to be accepted as you are, try to spot the problem the others are avoiding by their constant joking. Slowly, a bit at a time, see if you can get it out on the table, being alert to encourage the first people who begin to examine it openly. (Be prepared to object when someone else tries to punish the person who is serious by making him or her a target for humor.) But don't accuse people of having tried to suppress a problem with humor; this is something they will not be ready to admit.

It may take time for people to be willing to risk giving an honest, straight opinion. Unfortunately, they may display some temporary hostility toward you for pushing them in a direction they've been trying to avoid. But that is a price you must be prepared to pay if you don't want to perpetuate joking relationships.

Putting Down the Put-Down
Sometimes humor is obviously, pointedly used as a put-down. A consultant was lecturing to a group of managers from various organizations at a university-sponsored seminar. Apparently agreeing with some of the points the consultant was making, one manager said, "I'd sure like to see you come down to my company and tell our people these things. They could sure use it."

Smiling, the consultant said rather imperiously, "I'd be glad to. I might even knock some off my usual fees."

"Oh, you don't need to," the manager replied. "I have complete control over the petty cash fund."

Even the consultant had to laugh at the joke made at his expense. If you've ever experienced a public joke made at your expense, however, you may have found it hard to laugh at. You felt embarrassed, frustrated, and *stopped* by such a device, because the objective of the put-downer was not only to belittle you, but also to shut you off.

As a victim of a put-down, you probably noted at least three things about the situation.

You were embarrassed.

You felt the put-downer was trying to cop out or avoid dealing with an issue.

Unless you showed a determination to resist, *you didn't get much help from the others.*

There may be nothing you can do about the embarrassment, but if it happens again, you can rally support and keep the put-down artist from completely getting away with it.

Respond immediately to the put-down. Having it out with the put-downer is not generally recommended, although on occasion it can be strikingly effective. The problem is that your open, aggressive response could cause discomfort—especially if the group has tolerated put-downs to others. Your challenge may result in an attempt by one or more colleagues to move on to another, less controversial subject. Then, in effect, you will have been shut up twice.

Although aware of the possible consequences, you may still be willing to risk confronting your colleague in public.

Don't join in the laughter. When you do, you are sanctioning, or seeming to sanction, what has just happened to you.

Don't hide the fact that you disapprove of the put-down, but don't lose your temper, either. Undoubtedly other people are already embarrassed and your rage may push them to the limits of tolerance. They may try to isolate you, to keep you from being effective.

Use the right kind of response to nullify the put-down. For example, "I have the feeling I've been put down, and I'm wondering why."

You have been made the victim; you know it, the put-downer knows it, and everyone else present knows it. Therefore, acknowledge the fact and act the part. You may cause the put-downer to back off, even to apologize. And it's possible you may enlist an ally or two.

Have it out privately with the put-downer. If you don't want to respond to such rudeness in public, you might arrange to have a private talk with the offender. Tell the other person exactly how you felt when he or she put you down, sticking as much as possible to your feelings. Don't accuse the put-downer of trying to embarrass you or shut you off or of acting with malicious intentions. Such people can, and probably will, deny that was what they meant to do. If you confine yourself to telling them how you felt, they can't deny your right to speak up. They may try to rationalize, excuse, explain, but they can't dismiss your feelings.

What you've done is to put the other person on notice that you are not going to take future put-downs without some kind of response. And that notice may discourage any more attempts.

Ignore the put-down. When the put-down is a one-time occurrence, when it seems to indicate no malice on the part of the other person, when it is probably used just to close out discussion on an issue, then you may want to overlook it. This isn't easy to do, of course. Pride protests. But you may be able to score some points by getting the response you want. To illustrate, you are in a group, holding forth on a position or persisting in asking a question. Someone tries to poke fun at you for your persistence. You can say, "This is still not clear to me. Maybe it is to everyone else, and I'm the only one having trouble. If so, I hate to take up the group's time. Can somebody help me?" Put that way, you'll frequently get a constructive response from someone. You may find that others in the group don't have any clearer idea of the point under discussion than you do. Or you may find you *are* the only one who doesn't see the point, but that someone will try to explain, without rancor, what is unclear to you.

If you can keep your voice level and calm, your quiet dignity will go a long way toward disarming the person who tried to put you down.

While in most cases everyone present can recognize a put-down for what it is, that doesn't mean that it has been admired or accepted by others. Your response may have the effect of not only dampening the impact of this put-down, but also of discouraging such behavior in the future.

Dealing with the Public Attack

"Look, I'm getting sick and tired of your poking holes in everything that is said here. If you can't find some way of contributing to this session without shooting everyone else down, then I think you ought to get the hell out of here and let the rest of us get something done!"

Chances are that, at one time or another, you have been the victim of a verbal assault of this kind by an angry colleague. Regardless of whether or not you had done anything to provoke the outburst, the experience was probably painful. And embarrassing, especially if employees who report to you overheard the scene.

Even when you are willing to agree that the attacker has a legitimate complaint, you may get angry because you feel that the abuse is disproportionate to the seriousness of the offense. Consequently, you may be tempted to respond with some angry words of your own. If this is what you usually do, it probably won't have any effect. Nor will it make you feel better. It is just the repetition of a well-worn pattern, like the "you did so! I did not!" game children play. What are the other alternatives for responding to an attack?

Shrug it off. It's extremely difficult, if not impossible, to look unconcerned while someone is haranguing you. Or to look at the complainer without responding either verbally or nonverbally, by your facial expressions. And frankly, it's a tactic that usually doesn't work. Your attacker will simply intensify the assault, and witnesses will wonder how long you can pretend to ignore what is going on.

Replying with logic is one alternative. Well, you can try it, but in most cases, any kind of reasonable argument won't reach someone who is emotionally upset. You will be wasting your breath. In addition, you may actually intensify the other person's emotions because you are not playing the game according to that person's rules.

Concentrate on stopping the attack. At the moment you'll probably be more successful in putting a stop to the scene than responding to the argument. Your feelings are involved; the experience is painful. The only decent way to stop the shouting is to meet feeling with feeling. Your feelings should be expressed in a controlled way. You might say, "Look, I wish you wouldn't shout at me" (delivered in a low, earnest tone). Or, "I know you're upset. Let's talk things over privately, without the witnesses. I'd like a chance to work this out with you."

There are certain considerations that can be applied to most public conflict scenes. For example, the people who witness the scene will usually be distressed by any prolonged show of emotion. This is true even if they think that the angry tirade is justified. Also, people who keep their cool under a fiery and withering attack usually command the respect—no matter how grudging—of the onlookers. Finally, the victim who seeks to gain sympathy after an attack often garners a harvest of contempt instead.

In short, this is one situation where you will fare best if you resist the temptation to give as good as you get. Try to defuse the emotional quality of the situation and arrange a private talk with the other person. Then perhaps you can have a reasonably open discussion of what you did or didn't do wrong.

Try not to let too much time elapse between the attack and your talk with the attacker. If you delay, you'll worry too much about what will go on. Your other work will suffer. You'll be tempted to talk with others in the department, which may not be fair to the person you're angry with. So get it off your chest as quickly as possible, provided you've managed to calm down a bit. You need to express your anger, but you should have some control over what you say and do.

Have the talk in private, in your office or the other person's. Don't put either of you on the spot unnecessarily by letting others overhear your anger or complaint.

When you do meet with your attacker, consider that your goal is twofold. You want to get your feelings out of you, where they are doing no good, and you hope to persuade the other person to change the offensive behavior. Therefore, the most important thing to do is say how you feel about it.

Get to the point that bothers you. Don't back into the real issue by making small talk. When deep feelings are involved, trivial chatter looks contrived. It just prolongs, and even intensifies, the discomfort you both feel. Say something like, "I have a problem to work out with you," or "Look, I'm really teed off by what you did, and I don't want to be so angry about it. I think it would help if I talked it out with you." Stick to your feelings, your reaction. Don't get sidetracked by a discussion of the other person's motives, which can be denied. But what can't be denied is how you felt.

Try to act normally after your discussion. The first thing to do is to drop the specific matter. It may be that as a result of the talk your relationship with the other person may have changed. Don't feel that you are obliged to act very chummy, or very standoffish either. Try to get back on a balanced footing, and let the other person know that you're prepared to work as you did before the incident.

There'll still probably be some embarrassment, defensiveness, and wariness for a time afterward. But you will have managed to keep such residual effects to manageable proportions. And it's a lot better than wearing out your carpet—and maybe your stomach—by all that pacing and churning.

Getting the Attention of an Unwilling Audience

Recently a manager I know attended an industry-wide meeting at which some technological advances were aired. One of the new processes seemed promising; in fact, he thought it would have great application in an associate's operation.

When he described the process to his colleague, however, the latter showed little interest. He almost seemed to go out of his way to find reasons for not considering it. The first manager was chagrined. He felt that his associate was forcing him to sell the whole idea, and he didn't think he should have been put in that position. What he didn't consider was that such proposals are often regarded as threats. "This character is invading my turf," the colleague thinks grimly. "He's trying to show me up."

Of course, a manager presenting an idea to a colleague cannot help having some investment in it. When that person is you, and you encounter a negative reception, you may sense criticism of your thinking; it's only normal to feel let down. Very often you will encounter resistance just because you are an outsider. "After all, what does Sam [or Paula] know about the problems I have."

If you are like most managers, however, you are pretty well tuned in to organizational goals. That means you are not always thinking only of your own areas of responsibility. Undoubtedly you believe, and rightly so, that communication and collaboration are desirable, perhaps essential, between departments, as well as up and down the command structure.

Furthermore, there's a lot of ego gratification in having your ideas accepted by others. It's good strategy, too. You increase visibility, and you gain a reputation as someone who is aware of organizational needs. Understandably, then, you'll probably want to continue to share your thinking, even though you know there will be resistance.

To get around this resistance, you might say something like this. "I feel that I'm being put in a selling position, and that's not why I'm here. I just wanted to let you know about this procedure in case it might be of some benefit to you." One production executive tried that approach. Her resisting colleague, she says, turned red, stammered, then apologized for giving her a bad time.

Of course, there are alternatives to simply taking your lumps. For example, you can:

Let go a written blast to top management. You can tell them what kinds of mistakes are being made or what improvements could be made in the operations of others. But even if you substantiate all your claims with flawless logic and irrefutable facts, chances are your memo will not have the effect you want. In some organizations such a course would be considered an impolitic move, or at least a breach of manners. There are bound to be people who will leap to justify the way things have been done, or protect those responsible for the way things have been done.

Take the idea to your boss. This may seem like the long way around in your efforts to improve horizontal communication, but it could help create a more receptive atmosphere. Tell your boss exactly what you have in mind, and suggest a meeting with your boss' colleague and yours (at which, of course, you would be willing to explain the idea in detail). If such a meeting can be arranged, you will probably have an easier time of it than if you meet with your colleague alone. For one thing, you'll have the sanction of higher authority. For another, even if your colleague wants to be negative, he may hesitate to do so in front of managers who may be higher up in the organization.

Write an advisory memo for your boss. The boss can then determine whether it should be forwarded, to whom, when, and whether to present it casually at lunch or in a more formal private discussion.

True, along the way authorship may become obscured, or the memo may disappear altogether. If it does go higher, though, the implication is that your presentation of your ideas is getting endorsement by each manager who passes it on.

Send a memo directly to your colleague. This is a good move when you don't want to raise large clouds of dust and you don't want to invest much time. Describe the idea briefly and concentrate on the pluses. Let your associate understand that if he or she wants to pursue the matter further, you'll be willing to arrange something. Send a copy of the memo to your boss.

Cultivate an inside friend. Perhaps there is someone within the other department who could be influential in passing along some of the outside information. Of course, again the authorship will be obscured. The credit will go to the insider. But at least the information, seeming to originate "in the family," will be less threatening. It's a slow, cumbersome, roundabout way of getting changes, but it's better than no influence at all.

You can also activate the grapevine, but in such a situation the information is often too sophisticated for most people to understand, much less transmit. Grapevines are usually better transmitters of less specialized and more popular knowledge.

In all too many bureaucracies, unless there are effective, sanctioned communication channels across functional or departmental lines, it's very difficult for a manager in one department to have influence or make an impact on a manager in another. Head-on, completely open approaches get blunted rather quickly. A softer, perhaps more circumspect manner of communicating may be in order, even though it takes longer. Persistence, especially when it recognizes organizational realities, often pays off.

It's important to establish a favorable image in others' minds. For example, you as the unasked (or ignored) expert will find it easier to get your message across if you are known to be receptive to the thinking of others. Sooner or later— probably later—people will come to know who is on top of the needed information.

Making a Good Partner
Of course, the ideal working relationship among managers is collaboration. The word *collaboration* gets tossed about quite a bit these days. It's the opposite of *competition*. It is also different from *cooperation*, which indicates a willingness to go along for some reason—perhaps because the boss wants it that way, or because a person feels, "If I don't cooperate, I can't get what I want." Collaboration springs from different motives. When you collaborate, you invest yourself in a joint effort because you want everyone involved to get what he or she wants—and what you want. Collaboration further implies that everyone engaged in the project will retain so far as possible his or her means of achieving the goal.

And *that* is difficult.

Two managers in a highly technical organization have agreed to design a project group that will involve the expertise and personnel of both their departments. The first manager's preferred way of working is to write down a number of ideas, organize them, then pass them along to the second so that she can comment and criticize. His idea of collaborating is to pass pieces of paper, and ideas, back and forth until the two managers can fashion a program incorporating the best thinking of both. The second manager thinks they ought to sit down first and bounce thoughts off each other out loud. After a while, she feels, a consensus will emerge.

The first manager sends several memos to the second manager, but nothing happens. When the first manager asks for a response, the second says she wasn't sure whether she was to comment orally or in writing. Then the two of them try it the other way, talking together. The first manager, who fidgets, gives the second the impression that, after so much talking, he is ready to give her anything she wants just to get the session over. Both are unhappy. The project eventually is finished, but so are the friendly feelings between the two.

Partners in a collaborative effort usually make an unfortunate mistake right at the beginning. They assume that, because they have shown they want to work together in a joint project, they are truly equal partners.

If you are about to become involved in a collaborative effort with a colleague, you may face a difficult experience, but a very rewarding one if you succeed. To help you succeed, here are some pointers.

Expect that your methods will differ. How you will work together, when, what should come out of the working sessions—all have to be discussed. Person A puts things off until she feels intense pressure, then devotes 100% of her time and energy. B likes to plot each step of the way, finishing some parts as early as possible.

Make tentative suggestions. Before you start on the project is the time to discuss, to suggest, to negotiate. Put up trial balloons. "Here's how I thought we might begin. What do you think?"

You can hardly expect instant agreement. For one thing, you need time to develop mutual trust and respect. Each of you will have to try ideas and methods and be prepared to back off when they don't work.

Go slowly at first. Take time in the beginning to work through the difficulties of the relationship between you. If you don't, later you may have to stop some critical phase of work, in order to deal with problems that were ignored or suppressed at the outset.

Face problems immediately. Any suppressed feelings of tension and frustration will not only get in the way of doing the work but will probably come rushing out in a destructive scene that can impair the relationship.

Give feedback. You assume that your collaborator realizes how much you value his or her work. But your collaborator may *not* realize. As you progress through each unit or stage, try to get across the message you want to give. If the other person's work is good, express your appreciation. If it isn't up to snuff, and if you think it can be improved, be tactful but also forthright in making suggestions.

Let your manner show that you are always aware this is a partnership, not a "Me up, you down" situation. Ask that you also be told how you are doing.

What often happens is that you and your collaborator may have agreed to divide certain parts of the task. You finish your assignments and then are chagrined to find that your partner hasn't finished his. You may feel anger. "Look, we agreed that I would do this and you would do that. I have. Why haven't you?" Such a reaction may produce an interesting, even heated, discussion. But it won't advance understanding—or the project. Better in most cases to put your anger aside and ask, "How about my giving you a hand? Anything you'd like me to do?" Working is preferable to stewing.

At last, you may be privileged to enjoy the rewards of a

successful collaboration: the stimulation of bouncing ideas off each other, a project that is better in many cases than either of you would or could have done on your own, deepened respect, and a good working relationship for the future. That's a good reason not to look on your role in the collaboration as evidence that you have demonstrated superiority, even if you did do more than half the work. It's a natural and very human perspective on an association that you have largely carried. But if you convey to your collaborator and to others that you feel that way, you may ensure that your next joint effort with anyone will be turned into a competitive effort. Your "collaborator" will be loathe to see you *win*.

Generally people recognize that collaboration is extremely difficult. The person who transcends these difficulties soon becomes known as the person who can work with other people to get things done.

chapter 6 Working Effectively With Your Boss

Next to you, your boss is probably your most important asset, and next to you, potentially your most serious obstacle to success. The boss can be mentor, publicist, and counselor, to name just a few roles. Your most desired role, from your manager's standpoint and yours, is to be a valued assistant. You have much to say about that. Managers, by the very definition of the word, must manage people—and relationships. Those relationships extend upward toward bosses as well as outward toward colleagues and downward toward subordinates. Even managers who feel reasonably competent in their lateral and downward dealings with people experience a good deal of stress in their relationships with their bosses.

The upward relationship is highly charged emotionally. Resentment, frustration, and impatience may characterize it. Both the relationship itself and the subordinate's view of it are clouded by impatience to get ahead in the corporate hierarchy, envy of the person who has reached a higher rung, resistance to a surrogate parent-child association, or inability to judge realistically the boss' competence.

Taking the Measure of Your Boss

This inability to evaluate one's manager objectively is rooted in more than lack of experience or knowledge of what a boss really has to contend with. The fact is that subordinates often insist that their bosses be better than they need be. Why? Well, for one thing, the boss represents authority, and we have to make the boss look superior in order to justify to ourselves our submission to authority. This is not to make a case that the boss is always right. Nor for the other side, "The boss may not always be right, but he is always the boss."

It's a safe bet that your personal success is closely tied to the success of your dealings with your boss. In other words, in career terms, your boss is one of your essential resources. Whether you use that resource profitably depends in large part on how well you understand your boss. Therefore it's important for you to try to develop an objective view of your boss and your relationship.

Ironically, while good managers view their subordinates as individuals with their own goals and their own problems, they often fail to grant the same privileges to their bosses. Get behind the title and ask yourself, "Just how much do I know about my boss as a human being?" Most of us believe that a person's behavior, values, and attitudes are influenced considerably by upbringing, environment, education, etc. What do you actually know of your boss' background? Education?

Once you've developed a clearer personal profile of your manager, take another look at the professional side. How long has this person been with the organization? What route has he or she taken to the present job? What kind of frustrations or triumphs has the boss experienced? Has the progress been easy or difficult, slow or rapid? How do others in the organization feel about your manager—and why?

It's a truism that all relationships have two sides. Still, many managers, looking upward, seem to feel that all the frustration is on their side. The boss, by virtue of superior authority, could resolve all matters by fiat if he or she really wanted to. Subordinates forget that, aside from whatever limitations may be imposed by superiors, the boss' feelings and attitudes are also shaped by dependence on subordinates. As your own experience will tell you, a manager can often feel anxiety and insecurity from the simple fact of having to rely on others—subordinates—to accomplish the objectives of the operation.

Behavioral scientists investigating the frictions within a company often make use of lists of reciprocal attitudes to help them determine problem causes. You may want to try it yourself. Draw up a list of complaints you have against your boss. Then for each one try to list what your boss' related complaint would be against you. This shouldn't be just an exercise in imagination. If you really make an effort to be honest with yourself, you'll find that you have a pretty good idea of what about you bothers your boss, even though it may not be pleasant to admit it.

Once you've identified the friction points, ask yourself what you can do about them, and what you want to do about them. These decisions should be made in the light of the answer to another key question: Where is your boss going?

The familiar advice that the best way to get ahead is to make your boss look good is a misleading oversimplification. You'll get a much clearer perspective if you think in terms of where your boss is headed and what this will mean to your future. Generally speaking, there are three broad possibilities on the boss' track:

Up. When bosses are ambitious, effective, and clearly destined for greater responsibility, they look for subordinates who will play on their team. The employees must be willing to hitch their wagons to the boss' star. The reward can be the pleasure of being part of a fast-moving operation. The danger is that managers may lose their identity in supporting their bosses' careers.

Shelf-sitting. Although it is often hard for young, eager subordinates to believe, many people do reach the point in management where they have all the responsibility they want. Maybe they know they have all they can handle, shrink from competition, are marking time to retirement, or simply find outside interests more absorbing. Whatever the reason, they are satisfied with their present responsibilities. This can be frustrating to subordinates who want to get—and keep—moving.

On the other hand, these people are often ideal teachers. Since they are not preoccupied with their own ambitions, they have the time and the willingness to share their experience with subordinates, delegate freely, and even encourage experimentation. The boss on the move may not be able to tolerate mistakes; the one on dead center may offer a protected environment where mistakes lead to learning instead of disaster.

Backsliding. Many managers find it difficult and distasteful to accept the authority of a superior who seems to be losing his or her grip or who is becoming downright incompetent. "Why don't they [i.e., top management] get rid of the jerk?" they complain. Of course, it's possible that the slipping superior is the owner's relative. Much more likely, however, is an answer his subordinates find it hard to accept: From top management's viewpoint, the supposedly incompetent boss is doing an adequate job. That's why the road to ruin is lined with the bones of managers who thought they could take a shortcut to the top by slipping a knife between the ribs of the boss.

All bosses, "good" and "bad," create both obstacles and opportunities for their subordinates. The wise manager is one who can cut through his or her emotional reactions and assess the situation objectively. Given this person, this relationship, this organizational situation, where does my opportunity lie? While I am working for this person, what can I get out of it—mobility, learning, experience, visibility—that will make me more qualified for additional responsibilities and more likely to handle them well when they come? Both in terms of job success today and career opportunities tomorrow, that could be one of the most important questions a manager could ask.

Supporting Your Boss

Visibility is essential to promotability, and one way to invite the boss' attention, of course, is to keep him or her involved in what you are doing. Information encourages involvement. In the organizational world, information is gold. No boss ever has enough of it. Most often, though, a manager hears from subordinates about problems. Most bosses would enjoy being on the receiving end of something positive, or at least neutral, for a change. Good news is always welcome.

What kind of information can a boss use that people rarely think to offer? There are, for instance:

Copies of memos. Managers usually give some thought to whether the boss should view copies of memos sent to people outside the department. But they tend to overlook the fact that their managers may be equally interested in memos to people within the department—if they are complimentary or discuss an unusual task or project. A copy of such a memo does two things: it gives the employee additional recognition, and it links your name to successful, out-of-the-ordinary action.

Employee comments and suggestions. Some managers relay verbal complaints or suggestions from employees when they converse with the boss. Others, however, get better mileage by suggesting the employee write a memo on the subject to be forwarded up the line. They can offer solutions to problems raised or comment on the suggestion in their own covering note, giving (and gaining) recognition for the innovation and sense of involvement of individuals in their departments.

Meetings. Occasionally, when you anticipate an impressive show, tell your boss you think he or she would find the time well spent getting direct exposure to what is going on in your group.

There are some bosses to whom none of the above methods would be really acceptable. They would start wondering, "What's going on here? Why the sudden attention?"

Still, the principle of passing on information is always a good one. There are other, less direct ways to go about it as well. One is a periodic departmental round-up—a sort of newsletter to employees—which tells who is working on

what, recent achievements, future plans. Naturally a copy
goes to the boss.

Another is the departmental bulletin board. Here you can
post memos for others that reflect favorably on your
operation, complimentary letters from customers and clients,
newspaper clippings about the outside accomplishments of
people in the department. Don't limit information to rave
reviews, however; material gains credibility if complaints and
criticisms are also given some exposure.

Other ways to let your boss know of your abilities are:

Whether or not you have a Management by Objectives
system, work out additional, personal goals you'd like to
achieve. Discuss them with your boss periodically.

Keep your boss up to date on your learning achievements.
If you go to a seminar, take a course, attend a lecture or
meeting, or take a field trip, then incorporate a summary of
your experience in a memo. More important, show the
applicability of what you've learned to some phase of the
operations.

Try to meet with your boss at least once a week on a semi-
formal basis. That is, don't make it an obligatory conference,
but a meeting that you can fit without fuss or resentment into
the boss' schedule.

Talk about the progress you've made only when you've
actually made it, when you can show results in terms that are
clearly meaningful.

Don't assume that your accomplishments are all your boss
wants to hear about. A good way for him or her to absorb the
progress you're making is to hear some of the problems you
haven't solved.

Praising the Boss

A lot of managers hesitate to pay the boss compliments.

They may say that to praise the boss is apple-polishing, or
that the boss is supposed to do outstanding work. But when
the praise is genuine, it is a courtesy that everyone—a
subordinate, a peer, a boss—deserves.

Or they may object that it's presumptuous to praise a

superior, that the boss gets praise from his or her own boss. This is hardly a realistic attitude. Everyone criticizes those who are higher in the organization. Your boss knows that you judge his or her performance and behavior all the time. Why not let your boss have the pleasure of knowing when the judgment is favorable. You probably feel you don't get too much, or even enough, praise from your boss. Probably he or she feels the same way.

The most important aspect of praising the boss is positive reinforcement. It's a simple fact—so obvious that it is often overlooked—that telling people how much you like what they did is an excellent way to encourage them to do it again. A manager who wants a good working relationship with the boss has much to gain by keeping that fact in mind.

Getting the Boss' Attention

"What do you do with a boss who doesn't listen?" an accounts manager complained to me. She then went on to describe a frustrating experience she'd had recently—the result, she felt, of her boss' frequent failure to listen.

The first hint of trouble came when she handed her boss a written request for an expense advance. "It's for my trip to Atlanta," she explained. "Remember, we discussed it early last week."

Her boss looked at the note and shook his head. "I don't recall talking about any trip," he said suspiciously. "Are you sure?"

"Of course I'm sure. I told you I had received a letter from our reps down there asking for some help. Apparently they've run into a rash of problems on the new line and don't know how to handle them. So I suggested that I go down there, make some calls, give them a brief retraining session. And you said okay."

"I really think we ought to hold up on this," her boss said. "Maybe I should talk with Al Gordon first. Also..."

The accounts manager was furious, but she realized that there was no point in continuing the discussion. All she could do was call the reps, cancel the reservations, and try to figure out why her boss never listens to her, or at least can't seem to remember what has been discussed.

When managers complain that their bosses don't listen, there is always the unflattering possibility that they themselves are to blame. It may simply be that they don't say anything worth listening to.

There are times, however, when we all make it difficult for another person to listen to us. For example, we catch someone on the run. He has a million other things on his mind, or he is already late for an appointment, or he is still mulling over the last conversation he had. And wham! We hit him with a whole new set of ideas. Who can blame him if he doesn't listen?

Sometimes, too, we can get so involved with our skills as storytellers that we lose sight of the need to get the message across sharply and speedily. In an effort to build suspense and to let the listener know in endless detail just how clever we were in handling every development, we put him or her to sleep.

A third self-imposed obstacle is neglecting to indicate to the listener just how what we are talking about relates to him. For example, compare the following conversation openers. "You know, I was going through the accounts receivable department—I had to pick up a request form in distribution that hadn't been properly made out—and I happened to run into Jess Slade. And he said something interesting—we had been talking about...."

"Hey, I just heard something in accounts receivable that should make you feel very happy."

Now which do you think would command more attention?

How can you get your boss—or anyone else, for that matter—to listen to you? The techniques used by experienced salespeople provide some practical suggestions.

In order to get attention, a salesperson will often delay the start of the sales presentation. He or she warms up the prospect first, talking about things that will probably interest the potential customer—a particular book, the performance of an athlete, game scores, and so on. Only when the sales rep has the customer's attention does the sales story begin.

This casual prelude serves another purpose, too. It can clue you in to whether or not you've picked a good time for this particular conversation. If your listener seems tense or distracted, postpone your message, if possible.

Tell the boss what you're going to talk about. Give the punch line first. Then explain the subject clearly. After you've told your manager what you wanted to say, find a way to summarize the key points, the ones you want the boss to remember and consider.

Get response. You may be tempted to state the data in a nonstop fashion, especially if you are talking to your boss. If you go about it in that fashion, however, you won't know how much he or she has actually heard. From time to time, throw in a question. "When I first thought this was the way to do it, I began to wonder. Maybe such-and-such would be better? What do you think?" You can also come right out with a comparison or several choices, pointing out which you think best, and asking for a reaction.

Avoid questions that call for a simple yes or no. And if possible, don't settle for a simple answer. Your listener may say "fine" or "okay," but this is no guarantee that he has really heard what you were saying. Try to get him to elaborate as much as possible. The more he talks, the more he indicates how much impact you have had on him.

In closing, get action. If you want the boss to take action, ask him or her specifically to do so. It's all too easy for a person to put off doing something, particularly if he or she hasn't heard enough to be convinced action is necessary. Some suggested rejoinders:

BOSS: "Maybe I should talk to Ned about this."
YOU: "Great! Why don't I see if Ned can get together with us right now."

BOSS: "Let me get back to you on this."
YOU: "Fine. Why don't I summarize this in a memo to keep it fresh in your mind. I'll have it in your

hands in an hour. Now when can we get together again?"

BOSS: "I'll have to think about this."

YOU: "Sure. Is there anything in particular that is causing you to hesitate about making the decision now?"

After you've said and done everything you can, including a follow-up memo, you may have to face facts. Your message hasn't gotten across. The only thing you can do then is to repeat it, and repeat it, and repeat it, with all the good nature you can command.

After all, your objective is to get something from your boss—attention, a decision, approval for a project. If you avoid making him or her feel sensitive about the failing, if you set up a schedule of gentle but persistent repetition, chances are you'll get the job done eventually, if not right away.

Getting a Bigger Piece of the Action

You may find your boss is a bit stingy in letting you have more challenge. The reasons why many executives don't delegate are varied and complex. Some people are afraid to let a subordinate do a job for which they themselves are still responsible. They fear that the subordinate will not do a good job—or will do it very well indeed. Or perhaps the executives simply think no one can do anything as well as they. Some executives just don't realize that they fail to delegate.

There are ways you, as manager, can persuade the boss to delegate without trying to deceive him or her about your real intentions.

Find something new to do. It shouldn't be too difficult to find a problem or an area for which the boss has not assumed formal responsibility, has not established official goals. That way the boss can give you not only all the authority you need but the responsibility as well. Your manager's neck is not on the block if you fail.

Look for what the boss doesn't do well. You can hardly have worked with this person for any length of time without realizing he or she doesn't do certain things as well as others (or doesn't like to do them)—talk to outsiders, fuss with the budget, schedule assignments, etc. The boss will be relieved to have you take over.

Share credit. The essence of this approach is to go for a small piece of the action, even to be a silent partner. Be prepared to let your manager take the credit. Persistence and your willingness to take a back seat can pay off.

Whatever the method you employ, you should realize that the boss may have anxieties about what you are doing. So supply reassurance by taking these steps:

Agree on goals. Make sure that you and the boss are clearly speaking the same language about what is to be accomplished.

Outline methods. Until you have earned more complete trust from your boss, you would do well to describe how you mean to go about the job.

Keep checking back. Even though you have secured agreement on means and goals, you will be wise to let the boss know what progress you are making, to reassure that you are still on the plan you discussed, and to ask for any suggestions.

Maintain a low profile. One mistake you may make when you have finally succeeded in getting the boss to delegate is to broadcast the news that you, not the boss, are responsible for the success of a project. Don't broadcast. You may have to wait a while for the public acclaim, but gossip being what it is in most organizations, it will come.

Delegating to Your Boss

Delegation is not a one-way proposition. There are times when you should enlist your boss' assistance in a task. Many managers are naturally reluctant to take their problems or responsibilities to the boss for fear of giving the impression that they are not up to the demands of the job. But there are some circumstances where such upward delegation is not only sound but will even win your superior's approval. You might consider it under these circumstances:

When the procedure will benefit from the higher status. A long-time, valued customer complains about a service deficiency. You take care of the problem, but you think an acknowledgment from your boss would carry more prestige and more quickly soothe the ruffled feelings of your customer.

When it will praise or flatter the boss. Like everyone else, bosses like to be wanted and needed. Perhaps you as well as your boss have been responsible for an achievement. You are asked to talk about it in a meeting, and you defer to the boss.

When you gain the benefit of your boss' authority. "I'd rather you announce the new policy in my department," a manager tells his boss, "to make clear its importance. I suspect there's going to be some resistance, and coming from you, the new rule will be easier to take."

When the consequence of error may be serious. "Frankly, Mike, there's so much riding on the outcome, I'd prefer you make the decision on the final design of the product."

While upward delegation should be used sparingly, failure to do so when it is appropriate is just as unwise as excessive dependence on a boss. In this area as in many others, a manager learns by experiment to walk a fine line. You may have to be prepared to assure your boss, however, that you are not simply dumping the job on your boss' desk to get rid of it.

Going up the Line

No matter how supportive he or she may be, there are times when you have to go through your boss to get action further up the line. For example, suppose you want to make a large capital expenditure. Or you'd like to expand your operation. Or you want to arrange a joint effort with another department that is not under your boss' jurisdiction. These are matters that often require decision-making at a level higher than that of your immediate superior.

The further away from you the decision is made, the less control you have over what goes on. There may be extensive delays before any action is taken, since the schedules of several other people are involved. Understandably, their order of priorities is probably not the same as yours. And your boss may not be able to push—or may not want to.

Once you have a good reason to send waves up the line, there are a variety of steps you can take to get yourself as close to the decision-making as possible. The following are suggestions you might wish to make to your boss.

A meeting to present your case. Your aim, of course, is to set up a session to make sure you'll do the talking about your proposal rather than someone else. There's always something lost in the translation when another person has to speak for you. Of course, you have to proceed with tact. There may be good reasons, however, for your boss to welcome this direct approach. He or she may be too tied down with other matters to do your proposal justice. In any event, if there is a strong bond of confidence between you and your boss, you may get the go-ahead.

However, you want to do more than just talk. You want, if possible, to be there when the decision is made. To do this, you have to have all the facts and present them cogently and decisively.

Attendance at the deliberations. This technique to speed decision-making up the line is not as strong as asking for a meeting at which you do the explaining. However, you may find it a more diplomatic suggestion. At least you've provided the opportunity to get a meeting going, and you'll be there to see that everything you want said will be. Before the meeting takes place, discuss with your boss how you can be most effective. What kind of supportive role should you play?

A memo. This approach for stirring up the decision-making machinery is usually not as effective as participating in a meeting with higher managers. A memo can be set aside or buried; it doesn't have any great urgency about it. But it does give you a chance to get your ideas across in your own words. Address the memo to your boss to pass along; conclude with an offer to discuss the matter personally with anyone who wishes to do so.

If a decision is put off and your request goes into limbo, you may be looking for ways to reactivate it. Perhaps in your original request there was at least one selling point you left out. Or perhaps there has been an additional development that might affect your proposal. Anything in the areas of cost, application, newly discovered benefits, that could justify saying, "Here's something else that should be considered," can be used as a door-opener.

All the approaches mentioned involve a certain element of risk. You may get turned down on your efforts to get things rolling. You may even hasten a negative decision. But if you proceed tactfully, you should not worry about being considered pushy. After all, you are vitally concerned; people expect you to speak up.

Asking for a Raise

Perhaps the most important aspect of asking for more money is the work you do before you even approach the boss. It's important to do your homework carefully ahead of time, marshaling your ideas, putting them on paper, actually constructing a presentation.

The first question you must answer is this: Am I justified in asking for this raise? From the boss' standpoint as well as from my own?

Some points to put on paper are:

Specific objectives achieved versus objectives planned. You probably can't expect that all of your plans have been realized, but in terms of priority, how many of the really important ones have been?

Monetary savings, compiled in dollars and cents with, if available, comparable costs for previous periods.

Specific statistics supporting your claims of increased productivity, together with any evidence that the increased production has been closely and directly related to steps you have taken or changes you have instituted.

New skills mastered, new resources gained through training, that point to increased effectiveness of performance. There are two levels here; one has to do with your department, the other with you personally.

Savings of time—for example, goals reached ahead of deadline.

Any examples that indicate high morale and team consciousness or commitment to goals among the employees in your jurisdiction, such as voluntary overtime, innovativeness, response to crisis, etc. It may have been an outstanding effort at the time, widely recognized. But be prepared to refresh the boss' mind.

New developments and ideas that sound promising.

However, in all your planning, bear in mind that the boss will probably be thinking about the cost of your extra pay, and wondering whether it will be a worthwhile investment. If you list, for example, the most significant thing that you accomplished this past year, remember that it will be much more impressive if it was not a one-time correction or solution but rather an event that continues to produce benefits. What is past is presumably paid for. What is to come must yet be paid for, and if you can show that the future can be expected to be so much better than the past, then the investment in you should be proportionately higher.

Of course, one base for argument is the differential you can reasonably expect to enjoy between your pay and that of your top echelon of subordinates. Most organizations place great value on such a differential; it creates status, among other things. If, therefore, you have been vigorous in pursuing rewards for superior performance by your key people, then you have not only made it likely that management will see a need to increase your compensation, but you have drawn attention to your superior accomplishments as a manager.

One other point should be seriously considered before talking to your manager. How replaceable are you? Obviously how hard you push for the raise depends in large part on what you represent to the organization. It isn't enough to say they would have to spend such-and-such to hire someone else. A prime consideration is how much trouble the organization would have to find someone who could fill your shoes—how long would it take to recruit and train someone. Answering these things to your satisfaction will have an effect on how well you present your argument, how convincing you are.

It's a mistake to think only of the pluses, however. No matter how valid a case you can make for your department's superior showing, there are bound to be some weak spots. Prepare yourself for any objections. For example, if your department hasn't been as productive as you suspect your boss would like, or as was projected at the start of the year, be ready to substantiate any explanations you offer for the deficiency. There may be factors beyond your and your subordinates' control—inadequate equipment, economic conditions, suppliers' failures, market vagaries, etc. However, be careful not to point a finger of blame at others. There need be—and it's usually better if there are—no scapegoats.

Next, have a suggested solution ready for as many of these difficulties as you can reasonably be expected to solve with the time and resources available. Your case will be better if you can show how those solutions have already worked. At the very least, you can show cost-cutting steps you have taken to reduce the financial impact of the setbacks.

Don't waste time arguing against justified criticism. Concentrate instead on the future and what you and your group are planning to do to improve.

Even the best prepared presentation for the most deserved raise can meet with disappointment. If the refusal is tied to specific shortcomings in your operation, you know what targets to shoot for next year.

Timing the interview and request is very important to the success of your venture. Try to arrange your appointment so that you won't be rushed or distracted. Just before lunch or at the end of the day, or when the boss is due at an important meeting, are probably not propitious times. You want the boss' mind to be fully on what you say, and you also want sufficient time to discuss any reservations the boss might have. If your boss is an early and fast starter, first thing in the morning might be good.

How about over lunch? That's an iffy question. It might be construed by your manager as taking advantage of a social moment. If he or she has had something to drink, there's the possibility of indiscretion. For example, the booze and bonhomie might lead the boss into going along exuberantly. Later there might be some backing away, and some resentment that you trapped him or her. Or the boss might promise and immediately forget.

If a congenial opening arises before the appointment—say, if the boss sits down in your office for a relaxed chat, take advantage of it. That is, of course, if you've already prepared your story.

If possible, a face-to-face request is better than a memo. One executive I know wrote a detailed memo to her boss just before she left on a vacation. There would probably have been no problem as to acceptance of her request, except that while the subordinate was lying on a beach enjoying the sun, her boss was being told he was not going to get the promotion *he* had been anticipating. End of salary request.

If the boss indicates satisfaction with you, your performance, and that of your subordinates but says the matter of a raise cannot be discussed now, ask the boss to tell you what has to happen before the raise can be discussed, or when the two of you can sit down again to discuss the matter.

Protecting Yourself When You're a Protégé

Ever since Joseph interpreted pharaoh's dream and instantly became his right-hand man, it's been clear that one way to get ahead is to have a powerful sponsor. In many organizations, the middle manager will find it nearly impossible to climb high on the corporate ladder without a strong assist from someone on the upper rungs. In addition to achieving easier advancement, managers who have sponsors are protected from many of the slings and arrows their less fortunate colleagues have to endure. In fact, the very word "protégé" means "the protected one."

Managers who have sponsors in their organizations' top ranks should anticipate certain reactions among their colleagues and should be aware of drawbacks of their favored status.

You will be envied. This is an obvious hazard for anyone who has been singled out. If the day comes when the protégé is promoted to higher rank, getting the cooperation of those who were bypassed may be difficult. A likeable personality, good manners and, especially, demonstrably strong capabilities go a long way in keeping the natural envy of others from becoming vituperative. But you may also have to be much shrewder than your mentor at judging the political climate of the organization. The higher manager's sponsorship will seem—to him—sufficient to protect you. This won't necessarily be so at all times.

You'll need to stay alert. The fact that colleagues or executives on levels between you and your sponsor are obviously envious can become a handy excuse for shutting out what they have to say. Legitimate criticism, anything you would rather not hear, can easily be written off as sour grapes. If you begin to let that happen, then you are brushing aside opportunities to learn. While ignoring criticism is always harmful, it can become particularly so if, because of your mentor, you are promoted to a job for which you are really not well trained.

You may have to work to keep your identity. The protégé-sponsor relationship can, in fact, become very much like that of a parent and child. The junior person may turn into a replica of the "parent," losing the ability to respond to situations that the sponsor hasn't handled. In a world of rapid change, this rigidity has ruined the careers of many executives who seemed to have everything going for them, including well-placed parent figures.

It isn't easy to stand up to someone you respect who also

holds the key to your future. There will be times, however, when your judgment will be best. Don't be afraid to defend it. And be aware, in your own mind, of the distinction between your mentor's goals and yours; they are bound to differ in some respects.

There are at least three pitfalls from which even the strongest sponsor cannot protect a favored subordinate. Those who find themselves in the position of protégé, or who would like to be there, should never overlook the consequences of falling into these traps. First, if the sponsor doesn't work out, you will probably be asked to leave should that executive be terminated. Second, it may be impossible for you ever to rise above the sponsor's level, at least until his or her retirement. Third, when your mentor does retire and you are ready to step into his or her shoes, you may find that top management or the board of directors has other ideas.

Be sure to find ways in your job to make your own mark as an executive. Above all, avoid appearing as though your major ability lies in bolstering the sponsor's ego.

If it gets to the point that the relationship is no longer beneficial *to you*—and it won't be beneficial if you lose your self-respect—be hard-headed about it. Get out while you still can call your soul your own.

Despite the potential dangers, it is generally unnecessary for the manager to reject the interest and helping hand of someone "up top." The traps are there, yet anyone who continues to rely on performance for self-esteem and to build a solid basis for advancement, who maintains a sense of humor and of proportion, and who doesn't let the friendship get in the way of other, less exalted relationships, can usually manage to have the best of both worlds.

Looking Good to the New Boss

Shortly after Abraham Lincoln was inauguarated, his secretary of state, William Seward, sent the sixteenth president a letter in which he offered to relieve Lincoln of all major decision-making responsibilities. The president quickly put the brash cabinet officer in his place.

The scale of Seward's presumption is hard to match, and

few managers would be so foolish as to try. Nevertheless, when a new boss arrives on the scene, it is natural to be concerned about how your relationship with him or her will develop. It makes sense to shoot for a situation that will help you do your job more effectively, provide new growth opportunities, and increase your satisfaction in your work.

Here are some suggestions to help you pursue a policy of enlightened self-interest. Since timing is all-important, the suggestions are arranged approximately in the order they can be used.

Don't come on strong at first. There's usually an introductory stage for the new manager from another location or company. He isn't really into the learning phase yet. He shakes a lot of hands, hears a lot of names, but impressions are blurred.

Respect the pressure he is under. Everyone is trying to make a good impression, and he probably feels boxed in. Don't try to load him up with information or proposals for changes. Save your ammunition for the learning phase, when he is seriously studying the operation. That's when you want to become a valuable resource to him. Later, when he takes full charge of decision-making, he will regard you as someone he can trust to share some of his authority.

Be yourself. There's a temptation to make yourself look as good as possible with a new boss, perhaps even to the point of turning only your good profile. But if she is to work constructively with you, she has to know the extent of your knowledge and experience, your personality, your style, etc. She'll more readily accept you if she thinks she is seeing the warts, too.

Invite him to lunch. Don't assume that if your new boss wants to lunch with you he will say so. He may not want to seem to single anybody out by issuing an invitation, but may be happy to be asked. If you feel he may hesitate to join you alone, suggest a group luncheon.

One advantage of talking with a new boss in an informal atmosphere is that you can more readily ask about his background and experience. The more you know about what he did before joining your operation, the better you can understand his behavior and decisions later. Chances are, like most people, he'll find talking about himself very enjoyable.

Look for personal help you can offer. If your new boss has moved from a distance, you may find that she appreciates any suggestions you can offer on services in the area—doctors, dentists, butchers, good places to shop, plumbers, banks, credit to establish, places to see, etc. Your help may not have any direct connection with business, but it can establish you in her mind as a person who can be called on, who is thoughtful and generous.

Try to appreciate your new boss' problems before expecting help with yours. After all, you're familiar with your job, but she may be only learning—especially if she has been brought in from another company. She may know procedures, but she's unlikely to know how best to operate with the people in your company or division. This takes time, and you can help by solving your own problems whenever possible.

Keep communications open and explicit. Let her know what you're doing when she is ready to know. Remember, she is not familiar with your mannerisms. With your old boss, a gesture, a look, a tone of voice may have sufficed. But until you and your new boss get to know each other better, you'll have to lean heavily on explicit statements, written reports, and memos.

Tell him about the people in your department. After he has had some time to get settled in his new assignment, you might prepare a rundown on the key personnel in your department. This can help the new boss learn what human resources are available. He has probably seen the personnel files, so design the memo to update and fill out that information.

Even though the new boss may have been filled in by his boss or his predecessor about what is going on generally, ask employees who report to you to describe the work in progress in a memo—who is doing what, why, and how far along the work is. This may be an appropriate time to forward suggestions and grievances from the people who report to you. It is certainly a legitimate way to call attention to you and your operation, but sell softly. Write down everything you want him to know, since he will probably want to defer any extensive discussion.

Think about the best role for him to play. When a new boss arrives on the scene, he may be unclear as to how he should proceed during the leadership transition. If the department is long established (and the people, too), and if things are running fairly well, he may want to keep things as they are for a while. He can afford to.

On the other hand, if the department is demoralized and disorganized, if people are working at cross purposes, or if the department is filled with eager beavers who want to step up the pace, then a change of direction is indicated—and the sooner the better.

Your recommendations to the new boss should be based on the needs of the department as you see them. But be sensitive to resistance. He may have priorities you don't know about.

Invite her to your meetings. The new boss may not be eager to participate in your conferences, but give her the chance. That's a good way for her to become comfortable with your colleagues, and for them to get used to her. If she wants to talk a bit about the problems she sees and her objectives, so much the better. It will help people get an idea of what kind of person she is. It helps avoid the insecurity that often develops when people aren't sure what the new person is up to.

Tell him how he is doing, especially when he has earned praise. Some managers go to the extreme of letting a new boss work things out entirely for himself through trial and error. Others go to the opposite extreme and shower compliments and suggestions on a new boss, creating confusion and suspicion as to their sincerity.

The best advice is this: when the boss does something well

in your judgment, let him know you think so and why. When he does something wrong, don't rush to tell him. Your reticence may encourage him to ask how you feel about what he has done. Also, he may be operating from different data than you have, so what seems to be a misstep to you may not be wrong at all in a larger context.

It's a mistake to believe that good performance and a good record are all that are needed to be accepted as a valuable resource by any boss, especially a new one. It is also necessary to guarantee some visibility for yourself. If you handle it well, the new boss will probably appreciate it. He has probably done the same thing himself in the past and will understand your motives. He should care most about how much he can benefit from what you are doing. If you offer him assistance, collaboration, results, you are advancing his cause as well as your own.

All the superior-subordinate relationships described above have involved positive interactions of one type or another. Of course, it is just as crucial to be able to relate to one's superior in a situation involving differences of opinion, conflict, and confrontation.

Being Negative with the Boss

All things considered, praise or positive feedback may be easier to offer than criticism of the boss' action or decision. The boss is about to promote the wrong person, in your opinion. Or make a capital expenditure that you think is unwise. Or okay a project you think should be investigated more thoroughly.

Usually you don't rush to challenge a decision your boss has made. It may be wrong, but not so wrong that you want to make an issue of it. And for all you know, your boss may merely be carrying out a directive from higher up the line, and may also feel a mistake is being made. If so, he or she may not welcome any suggestion that the decision is a bad one.

Nevertheless you feel you have to speak up, because the mistake will hurt you. The damage will be done in an area for which you are accountable. After all, there's your career to consider as well as your boss', and there are people working for you who may be hurt.

You're expected to help your boss look good. You really aren't doing your boss a service when you fail to point out that the decision is wrong. To go along with a decision that you know is wrong is closely akin to what is called malicious obedience. It won't benefit you, or your boss, either, to carry out a course of action that you know and hope will later cause the boss embarrassment.

Once you've decided to challenge a decision, what's the most effective way to go about it? Here are points to consider:

Your approach. Perhaps the last thing your boss wants to hear at this point is an objection from you about a decision he or she is already committed to. Perhaps your relationship, though, is such that you can be direct.

However, to avoid unpleasant reactions, you might ease into the discussion. "Something's been bothering me about Carl's promotion. I can't get it out of my head that we ought to hold off another few days and review the options again." Whether or not the boss appreciates your gambit, your tact may permit you to reopen the discussion.

If your relationship doesn't require this sort of roundabout approach, however, then there's no reason why you can't tell the boss candidly how wrong you think the decision is.

Your options. It's usually not a good idea to confront your boss with the possibility (or the veiled hint) that you'll go over his or her head. For one thing, there's little chance that such action will get you what you want. But it's another matter to raise the possibility that you can support your criticism with the kind of facts your manager can take to higher management. After all, it's your best bet to assume that the boss is as much interested in correcting a potentially damaging decision as you are.

Your limits. The case is a little different when your boss has already implemented the decision. Commitments have been made, requisitions have been drawn up, funds have been allocated and accounted for. To reverse the decision would mean undoing a great deal of work. Any objection you make at this stage will have to be serious and well documented. Establish in your mind a point beyond which you won't push, a point at which no real gain will be realized by reversing the decision.

Suppose nothing changes? You've made your objections, perhaps even written a memorandum. By doing so, you may or may not have enhanced your reputation and/or your future with the company. But the decision remains unchanged, and you must live with it.

In this case, it's worth remembering that a well-reasoned objection can often do more for your status with your boss than any number of agreements. True, you may not have won your argument, but having had the courage to make it gives you a much better chance of being taken into the decision-making process next time.

Complaining to the Boss

What do you do when the boss has commended you, promoted you, or given you a raise? Well, there is probably no harm done by your praising the keen insight, sense of fairness or executive ability behind that action.

But what do you do when you are disappointed, surprised, or angered by some action of your boss? Undoubtedly you don't feel the same freedom to criticize as you do to praise. You can, however, respond rather than turn bitterly away. Here are some suggestions for getting results.

Focus on the facts. If you've been handed an additional assignment at a time when you're already up to your neck, center the discussion on your work load. It is tempting to talk about how much you're doing and the lesser amount done by a colleague. Unfortunately, that may merely lead the boss to defend the other person's work load without changing yours. Besides, a charge of unfairness, whether stated directly or implied, is not likely to change anyone's mind. The boss has probably given a lot of thought to what's fair, just as you do when apportioning responsibility.

Just lay out the evidence. The new responsibility will add a full day's work to what is already a full week's work. You don't see how you can manage it—not if you are to maintain your usual high quality.

Even when you feel injured by a decision, keep the heat out of your comments. If, for example, you get a memo on overtime costs that lists your group as the biggest spenders, you may feel hard done by. After all, your warehouse is a service unit that responds to the demands of other departments. Your people have been working extra hours simply because other managers have not been properly anticipating their needs. In justice, they ought to be charged with your overtime costs.

That is best discussed without heat, and as part of a suggestion to the boss that perhaps you can get together with the other people involved to solve the problem. In fact, if you were to work out the problem first and present the solution to the boss, instead of a complaint, that would be an even better procedure. Indeed, that may have been in the boss' mind when the memo was sent.

Don't fight a decision you don't like before asking why. A promotion to division manager has gone to a colleague whose work isn't as good as yours, but who is a better politician. At least, that's your view. What you want to know, if you decide to question the boss' choice, is primarily why you didn't get the promotion, not why the other person did. You may agree, when the boss has explained why you're not quite ready. You may see the boss' rationale, even if it hurts.

On the other hand, you may still not agree. You may be convinced that you've been unfairly treated. All you can do is restate your case, then wait and see what happens next time. While you are waiting, the time is best spent improving in the areas your boss suggested need work.

Often when you complain you find that the boss had little idea you felt the way you do or that you were interested and involved in the matter. Complaints and negative responses are therefore useful in increasing your visibility and establishing your profile in others' minds.

Protecting Yourself in a Conflict with the Boss

How do you protect yourself when you find yourself in a conflict with your boss? Or when you and your boss just aren't getting along too well? Consider these ideas:

Shoot for success. It's hard to fault it. The safest way to protect your position is to make it tops at your own level. You need your subordinates' help in this. Even if you can't give the extras that make them push a little harder, you can appeal to them in other ways. One is to let them guess, carefully and without saying anything that will later embarrass you, that you have a problem. "Despite all we've done—or maybe because of all we've done—there's pressure on me for more. I think some people think we can't do it. We can, if you believe it."

Cut no corners. Don't invite trouble by violating rules, even if they usually aren't enforced. You can be sure you're being watched. If you're running your group on a little more overtime than is authorized to get the job done, get it done without it. You don't want memos that "bring the policy to your attention" building up in your file. Or if you are freer than the rule book recommends about R&D work or the level of expense allowances, because it's good for morale, keep your people happy another way.

After all, if they appreciate what you do for them, they'd hate to lose you altogether.

Acquire allies. Among your colleagues there may be some who won't be a bit upset about your problem. But what about the others? Do they share your opinions of the superior in question? If they do, and their feelings toward you are positive, they can be useful allies. They can be alert to what the grapevine says your boss is saying or planning, and warn you. They can also influence their bosses in their thinking about your situation.

Cultivate higher management. If ever there was a time to cultivate the person at the top, this is it. If something special happens in your group—the biggest sale of the month or the fewest number of rejects in two years—send a note of congratulations to the person responsible and a copy to your own Mr. Big. "Thought you'd like to know what we're doing here...."

This is a good time to rack your brains for an innovative suggestion to pass on for what it's worth. The commander-in-chief, after all, is the best friend at court you could have.

All of the suggestions above, while useful, still leave you in a largely defensive stance. More than that, they can take the joy out of your job. Isn't it also conceivable that your superior doesn't like this game either?

How would it be if you sought the boss out, talked it out, pledged your efforts to work through it?

Using Clout

No doubt in dealing with your boss you sometimes wonder how much influence—translate *power*—you really have. And you may on occasion be tempted to find out.

Just as an experienced lawyer will not ask a question in the courtroom unless the answer is pretty certain to be favorable, a management tactician does not try to exercise clout unless there's a very good chance the show will be effective. It's wise to avoid the risk of demonstrating too little strength.

In cases where a decision of great impact is in the making and your emotional reaction is high, you'll find it best to try to suspend the discussion and reschedule it. Use any reason. "Look, this is pretty heavy. Mind if I take some time to digest it? Can we talk about it tomorrow?" Or even, "I'm right in the middle of a job. Can we talk later?"

The important thing is to have time and a cool head to be able to look at the available options. If you think you have only one option, which is to go for broke, that's usually the time you should *not* act. Once you have won time, you can:

Drain your emotion. You may even want to go outside for a walk, or to talk to someone. Put some distance between you and what is troubling you.

Get facts. Chances are that in the heat of emotion you heard too few of them. Put down all the questions you can think of. Then you'll have an agenda, a track to run on, when you get back to the boss.

Measure your power. If you think a confrontation is brewing, find out how much clout you have before showing it. How valued are you by higher management (other than your boss)? How replaceable are you? How is your boss regarded in the organization? The answers may tell you how far out you can venture.

Outline a presentation. It doesn't have to be formal. Probably in most cases it shouldn't be. But what you need are facts or data leading to a certain conclusion. Try to get to keep the subjective, biased element out of it as much as possible. Avoid "I think" or "In my opinion..."

If you don't make headway, you may then want to consider making predictions or issuing an ultimatum. However, this assumes that you have measured your strength and feel you have considerable power. It's also possible that during the cooling-off period, you decided that the consequences will not be so devastating after all.

If you decide you have to go for the grand gesture, do it quietly but firmly. What you want is a believing audience, not someone who feels outraged to the point where he or she automatically defies you.

Before you make your gesture, however, whether it be a strong statement or a threat to quit, consider:

The cost may be too great. Even though you have tried every conceivable way to get done what you feel needs to be done, and your attempts have failed, make sure you understand the implications and costs of what you are contemplating. What will it mean to you in terms of your career and your continuing relationships with others at work, your family and home life, and your self-respect and the respect of others? Finally, what are the chances of getting the results you hope for? Only after asking yourself these hard questions will you be able to determine whether the costs of your proposed dramatic gesture are worth paying.

You may lock yourself into a situation and not be able to turn back. A typical dramatic gesture is the demand "Either he goes or I go." In the heat of anger, people frequently see a situation in black and white. The choice appears simple, but situations are seldom so well delineated. There are usually varying shades of gray that suggest less radical solutions. If you issue an ultimatum and lose, you may be stuck with it. One manager who announced he was quitting later regretted what he had done, but when his boss made no move to talk him out of it, the man felt he had to proceed with his resignation.

chapter 7 Dealing With Conflict

A colleague of mine once went to a workshop on conflict resolution sponsored by a local university. The participants formed small groups to discuss a controversial issue and observe how they handled the inevitable conflicts. But in my colleague's group, there was no disagreement. "We agreed on everything we discussed," she reported. Only later did she realize that the members of her group had made an implicit contract among themselves that they would avoid any issue or statement that might produce conflict. They would discuss only "safe" subjects. No doubt these workshop participants exhibit the same kind of behavior at work.

It has been traditional in some organizations to believe that managers should try to conceal their negative feelings and deal with people and problems in as objective and rational a manner as possible. If any feelings are expressed, they should be positive—friendly, enthusiastic, good natured. Negative feelings—fear, hostility, guilt, anger—should be firmly suppressed. In many cases managers do not even admit to themselves, let alone to others, that they have such feelings.

To some, this sounds like common sense. It seems obvious

that expressing angry, unkind, or unfriendly feelings is unlikely to be helpful when people are trying to work together toward a common objective. But in recent years behavioral scientists have built up some pretty convincing evidence that this "common sense" about expressing anger and conflict is, at best, an oversimplification.

For one thing, a feeling doesn't go away simply because it is not voiced. It remains, and influences the person whether he or she admits it or not. "Jones and I just don't seem to see things the same way," can often be translated as, "I don't like Jones."

Secondly, the fact that a feeling is not spoken does not mean it is not expressed. Facial expressions and other behavior get the message across pretty clearly without words.

The result is that conflict exists, but in an unadmitted and unarticulated form. People fail to communicate, to cooperate, and do not understand why they have failed. Since the existence of conflict has never been admitted, the problem cannot be dealt with.

Admitting Conflict

What happens if anger and hostility are expressed, if a manager acts as he feels? Here's an example:

Two managers are having an argument. The company controller has just lost his patience with the operations chief and accused him of attempting to cover up a cost discrepancy in one of his departments. The supervisor who heads that department is a former college classmate of his boss, the operations manager, and was brought into the company on the latter's recommendation. Here's how the argument is going:

"I'm tired of you and your buddy playing games with me," says the controller angrily.

"Games?" the other man responds. "I resent that. I resent it very much."

"I don't care if you resent it or not," retorts the controller. "You're stopping me from doing my job."

And so it goes. The issue is out. The upshot? Eventually,

Operations no longer tries to protect his buddy (and, incidentally, himself), and the controller gains a much clearer idea of what's really happening in the company. So, consequently, does the person to whom he reports—the company president. And since accurate information is the basis of all good judgments, the company has a better chance at being profitably run.

It's a story with a satisfactory ending, at least from the profit point of view. But what about personal relationships? Have battle lines now been drawn between the two men? Are they no longer speaking to each other? Has infighting between them at the conference table been on the rise? Has one man determined to rid himself of the other?

The answer is no. True, the operations chief was rather distant toward the controller for a couple of days, but the two men must work together too closely to remain hostile. Besides, the operations chief realized the essential justice of the controller's position, that he had been overprotecting his classmate. Subsequently, he and his buddy had a showdown of their own—one that cleared the air and enabled both men to do their jobs better.

Willingness to do battle when it is necessary is a form of honesty. This is not to say that the person who is continually expressing hostility in one form or another is being genuine. Rudeness, for example, only drives people away. Such behavior is usually the result of anger that wasn't directed where it should have been—at the person who incurred it— and is now misdirected to the world at large.

It's pretty obvious, for example, that people who spend their waking hours talking about their manager's loathsome behavior are doing so because for one reason or another they are afraid to tell the boss directly how he or she has done them wrong. (They may have good reason to be afraid; their boss may be the type who can't express anger and can't tolerate it in others.)

When anger is tolerated, there's usually a good working climate because conflict is brought out in the open where it can be dealt with and resolved. When anger is concealed, the unadmitted conflict continues and festers.

This is why it can be wise, although not always pleasant, for managers to encourage subordinates to express their negative feelings. There are areas of disagreement that need more than cordiality or even reason if they are to be resolved. The manager who allows disputes, however heated, to be expressed may be able to reduce the amount of hidden, unresolved conflict.

There is no question, however, that the use of anger can cause problems, especially when you don't handle it very well. Here are some suggestions on how you can express hostile feelings with constructive results.

Give fair warning. One of the biggest problem-causers in dealing with other people is anger expressed when the other person has no idea it is coming. Most of us have had the experience of offering what we considered constructive criticism, only to have the other person blow up in our face. The unexpected anger makes us want to avoid any contact with the person who blew up at us, even when it's advantageous to maintain contact.

This is why it's often necessary to deliver what amounts to fair warning of the way you feel. A simple phrase like, "This is starting to irritate me," or "I'm feeling very angry," can be very helpful. What isn't helpful is to maintain a facade of so-called rationality while your voice, your gestures, or other physical signs not only give away your real feelings, but aggravate them as well.

Be specific. No matter how a dispute starts, it is likely to be painful. But it can also be profitable, providing both you and the other person find out what's really bothering each other. State immediately, in as few words as possible, just what it is that's making you hot under the collar. (If you can't do this, your problem may not be as pressing as you think.) Repeat the cause of your anger frequently, with simple variations in the wording, until you're absolutely certain that you're being understood by the other person.

However, don't use the occasion to drag in a list of past, unresolved irritants. You want the other person to change the annoying behavior. It's doubtful he or she will be willing or able to change if buried under an avalanche of grievances.

Accept differences. Do not demand anger as an appropriate response to your own. Conversely, try not to answer anger with anger.

Listen. If the other person does get angry, try to make an extra effort to listen. Like you, he may be too excited to be as articulate as he should, and it's up to you to sort out the causes of his anger.

Try not to judge motivation. It's enough to say that what the other person has said or done has angered you. He or she can't deny your feelings. If you say something like "You've been looking for a chance to trip me up for weeks now," the other person may deny the accusation, and the two of you might never reach an understanding.

Benefiting from Conflict

It's probably unrealistic to strive for too much harmony in an organization. There is a need for disagreement as well as cooperation. Conflicts and partisanship can be a sign of organizational vigor; they mean people are pushing their ideas and innovations. Strong people are competing with one another for executive positions. One manager who believes another's policies and practices are harmful is trying to neutralize them for the overall good of the organization. When managers assume adversary positions, they make it less likely that important issues will be glossed over. If a genuine exchange of ideas takes place, there is less likelihood of organizational or managerial obsolescence.

The adversary style can be overdone, however. People can be so busy operating against each other that they get in the way of organizational objectives. Some of the danger signs:

Withholding information. People use information to increase their own power, not to help the operation run more efficiently.

Win/lose strategy. When a boss feels the most important thing is to look better than a peer, a subordinate, or even a higher executive, that can become a more important objective than any the organization has set.

Management style. Some managers become devil's advocates. Co-workers eventually get so used to the controversial stance that they discount it. These managers are then no longer taken seriously when they raise objections.

While excesses such as these should not be encouraged or rewarded, neither should you strive for constant unanimity. Some questions you might ask yourself are:

When was the last time you publicly recognized and approved of a subordinate taking an adversary position on a new project or proposal?

When was the last time you signaled to your staff that you don't want them to speak with a single voice?

How often have you shown that innovation counts with you in evaluating subordinates' performances?

If one manager fought against another manager's ideas, would you provide support for the challenge, even if co-workers reacted negatively to having the harmonious atmosphere disrupted?

These are a few of the ways you can signal to subordinates that, while you want them to support each other and collaborate, what is most important is to reach organizational goals, and doing so may require that some people challenge the ideas and actions of others.

Avoiding the Suppression of Conflict
In nearly every organization there are people who attempt to suppress any disagreement. They may be well intentioned, but the result is often to delay the resolution of arguments, leaving the participants fuming beneath the surface. An analysis of their techniques shows how this works.

"*Keep calm.*" When voices begin to rise, count on this person to try immediately to get everything back to normal, displaying a certain air of moral superiority over those who are arguing. But the sheepishness of those who are told to calm down usually inhibits any real progress in a discussion after that point, although the conflict is still boiling inside them.

How do you deal with the habitual keep-calmer? Try saying firmly, "No." If necessary, add, "I'm furious and, what's more, I think I have a right to be furious," explaining what has aroused your anger. Once you've got it out of your system and given others a chance to know your feelings, a rational give-and-take is much more likely.

Picking the winner. Some people habitually try to end any conflict by coming down as soon as possible on the side with the most power. They will do so even when it involves taking a position completely at variance with what they have said in the past or with commitments they've made privately.

Obviously such "peacemakers" make poor allies. They are only warm bodies on whatever side appears to be backed by the boss or someone else with clout. Among equals they may switch back and forth in the course of a single meeting.

If you have something worth saying, it is important not to let the peacemaker cut off debate by trying to push you into the position of a helpless minority. Address the whole group and say something like, "If I'm in the wrong, let me know and I'll shut up," then present your arguments. If your points are well taken, others will probably want to explore them even if they do arouse strong feelings.

Defining the conflict in abstract—and patronizing—terms. At a meeting called to decide how to proceed with some necessary staff reductions, one executive sat in silence. Then something set him off and, voice raised, he expounded his view.

When the torrent slowed, another manager interjected with a condescending smile, "It's obvious that what we are really hearing is compassion, not realistic business practice."

Like that manager, some people who seek to end any conflict as quickly as possible have found that denigrating an opponent's arguments is one way to squelch that person. The other participants will then be too embarrassed to continue the discussion.

Fortunately, in this case, the first manager refused to accept the put-down. Admitting that he felt strongly about the matter, he also pointed out that he had raised some facts that needed debate for the long-term good of the organization—a comment that won him immediate support from others. The meeting then continued.

Peacemaking is often constructive. Personal feuds may disrupt meetings, wasting the time and exhausting the patience of participants who aren't involved. Too, there are people who are simply feisty, looking for a bone of contention where none exists. But the habitual peacemaker should be examined closely. Although few people really like conflict, most recognize that it is one way legitimate disagreements emerge and are settled. The person who always seeks to hush a conflict creates a problem that may go unrecognized because seeking peace is considered a virtue in our society—it is the fighters who must be at fault.

If you find that important issues are not being fully debated because one individual continually seeks to turn off the discussion, here are some suggestions you may want to follow.

Explain firmly but calmly why the debate must continue. Point out that you feel what you have to say is important, and that you want to hear what others have to say as well.

Recognize that the peacemaker probably feels threatened. Those who cannot stand conflict have some fear that may be deeply ingrained in their past. It's not your job to be a psychoanalyst, but you can still take that threatened feeling into account. Modulate your tone of voice; don't glare or act as though your opponents were deadly enemies.

At the end, show that there are no hard feelings. Peacemakers can be so upset by conflict that they are incapable of seeing the value of resolving the issues at hand. By speaking to their emotions, you may help them accept the need for argument.

One way to do this is to take pains, at the end of each conflict, to indicate that you have no grudge toward your opponents. Smile, behave normally. In other words, make it clear that conflicts are to be expected, and serve a purpose.

Using the Confrontation Technique

When conflict erupts between two key subordinates, many executives bring the two people together, face-to-face, to thrash things out.

Confrontation can be most effective. However, it may sometimes have effects that the unwary manager has not anticipated. Positions harden; hackles rise; arguments become defensive; logic gives way to attack. Labor mediators know this. That is why they may meet separately with the contesting parties for days on end before bringing them together.

Three basic problems come into play when adversaries face each other.

Perception. Each of the parties sees things differently. One side stands upon a set of "facts" and believes in those "facts." But the other side may present "facts" that are diametrically opposed. These opposing views are not accepted by the first side as facts; they are seen as arguments, often fallacious arguments. People do not abandon their perceptions when someone else presents opposing facts; each side continues to believe its own interpretation.

The game ethic. Most good poker players bluff in a game. Business psychologists have concluded that, in a confrontation situation, the game ethic often takes over. The adversaries bluff; they tend to move toward extreme positions, not toward each other. They become polarized.

Status. Once polarization has set in, people tend to freeze their positions. To modify the position would be to back down, give in, lose face. The risk of losing face seems to outweigh all other elements in the situation, even cold logic.

What can you do to avoid a destructive confrontation, one that makes things worse than they were before?

First, like the labor mediator, you can work with the disputing parties separately, exploring the facts of the situation. You'd be well advised to move in on the dispute before the opponents have taken public stands from which they'll find it hard to back down. Find out how each person sees things, and when he or she isn't seeing them plainly, point it out. The subordinate is much more likely to accept a clarification and modification of his or her "facts" from you than from an opponent. If you handle this preliminary exploration skillfully, you may well find that there is no need for confrontation.

Then formulate a solution that you believe each disputant can live with. Try it on each separately. Try to handle the discussion slowly and in steps, so that the person can adopt your solution as something he or she has come up with.

If it is not possible to reach this kind of separate agreement, then you may well feel that the confrontation is called for. Sit in on the confrontation, not as a neutral referee who breaks clinches and prohibits rabbit punches, but as an interested party. Your interest is the welfare of the organization—and of the disputants.

When you see the adversaries moving further apart, hardening their positions, move in. Look for any area of agreement to keep avenues open, to provide room for face-saving gestures, to prepare the way for your own solution, if necessary.

Bringing people face-to-face with each other to solve a problem can sometimes be avoided. If unavoidable, it should be preceded by constructive spadework. And when it happens, it should be controlled. Uncontrolled, head-knocking confrontation sometimes happens no matter what is done to prevent it, but it is hardly a preferred course of action.

Developing Relationships by Objectives
The Federal Mediation and Conciliation Service has developed a successful technique for use in labor-management

disputes. It's called *Relationships by Objectives* (RBO), and executives who must resolve other kinds of conflict involving themselves or others may well find it helpful.

Usually, each person or group involved in an argument spends valuable time pointing out what went wrong and particularly who was to blame. Once the cause and the culprit have been identified, progress stops—if it ever got started. The problem remains.

RBO is a technique to get some real movement started, and to keep it going until the problem is resolved. The idea is to get the adversaries to agree on certain common objectives and how they can realize them.

Suppose you have two highly valued managers, George and Susan, each heading a department that processes insurance policies. Policies with special riders have to be routed from George's group to Susan's and back again. Each department has a set of procedures that is logical in terms of its own operation, but the two sets don't mesh. Consequently there are constant squabbles over backlogs and delays in the work flow.

To use RBO in settling this dispute, you would ask George and Susan to follow these basic steps:

Get the data. You might suggest that the two managers (or two teams, one representing each department) sit down in a quiet place and answer two questions: What should the other department be doing to improve cooperation between us? What should we be doing?

Once you have the answers, you ask both managers or both teams to help you make up four lists.

1. According to George's department, Susan's group should...

2. According to Susan's department, George's group should...

3. According to George's department, George's group should...

4. According to Susan's department, Susan's group should...

Edit out complaints and finger-pointing so that you have

only positive statements. "He should stop doing..." becomes "He should start doing..."

Define common goals. Now call upon both sides to help you boil down the four lists into one—the objectives both managers (or teams) can agree on.

In George and Susan's case, the goals would be changes to improve the work flow so that each department has an equal burden and equal benefits. The teams might also consider ways to dissipate the bad feeling that has grown up between the two managers and the two groups.

Set specifics. Pick the goals that everyone agrees should have the highest priority, and decide how they will be achieved. For example, should a joint committee be formed to work out the new procedures for George's and Susan's groups? Should interdepartmental classes be organized to acquaint employees with the new methods? If so, who will conduct them?

At this stage, there are three requirements for the RBO technique to succeed:

A *specific outline* of what has to be done, step by step.

A *schedule showing* when each step should be accomplished.

Who will be responsible for seeing that it is done.
FMCS mediators hold automatic 90-day follow-ups to see that the steps agreed on are actually carried out. That's a good idea in resolving most kinds of conflict, to see that they stay resolved.

Managers often spend time looking for ways to restore the status quo. This is often a mistake, because problems provide opportunities. A dispute—whether it's horizontal or up-and-down in an organization—gives the people involved a chance to find new ways of talking about and doing things.

Deciding Whether to Intervene in a Feud
There are conflicts between employees that are not so much

problem-centered as personality-oriented. If you like both subordinates, you may wish they liked each other.

Of course, when one person is clearly in the wrong and the other is in the right, a manager may feel compelled to intervene, to act as judge. But when neither employee is right or wrong, when the feud is based on personal dislike or an old grievance, you must follow other guidelines.

Don't take sides. When the complaints you hear from employees in conflict are general ones, you may feel tempted to simply agree with whoever happens to be speaking at the moment—to nod or otherwise indicate that you are in sympathy. This is particularly true if you like the person, or find even a grain of truth in the complaint. On the other hand, if personally you and the employee are not close or if you feel he or she is being unfair to the other person, you may be tempted to disagree.

But it is best to let the employees work it out themselves, without your implied support of one or the other. The person whose side you endorse might use your agreement as a weapon. Worse, if you have the trust of both people, joining the feud could jeopardize your own effectiveness with them, and perhaps cause you to lose a valuable subordinate.

Judge the issue, not the people. There are times, of course, when you will have to make a judgment about a work-related quarrel. If you decide one way, you will seem to be boosting one subordinate; if you decide the other way, your action will be interpreted as supporting his or her opponent. Try to keep personalities out of the decision. Judge the merits of the arguments alone. Try not to let the possible political repercussions of your choice influence your action.

In announcing your decision, try as much as possible to make both people aware of the real, work-related reasons why you made your choice. This minimizes your personal contribution to their war.

Don't extend favors to one of two feuding employees. The minute you extend any sort of favors to one over the other, you are, whether you mean to or not, taking sides in their conflict. Such favors can vary from seemingly innocent pieces of information—advance notices, in-depth backgrounds, supplementary information—to access to additional secretarial help, or to the bending of rules and procedures for special situations. If you must offer such a benefit to one, make sure the other understands it is available to him or her as well, should the need arise.

Don't speak for one to the other. This is another way a manager can unwittingly get caught in the middle between two antagonistic subordinates. One may be talking to you about something the other did or said. You feel the critic is being unfair, so you try to justify or explain the other person's actions or words. In the process you can't help but inject your own understanding of what one disputant meant. This may or may not be what the person actually meant, and in any case, it may be offensive to the critic. You are only complicating the misunderstanding. A better course might be to indicate to the person complaining to you that he or she really ought to take up the matter directly with the other person, and let that employee speak for himself or herself.

Concentrate on their behavior, not their feelings. If the war between two employees is adversely affecting the work of either, you may feel you should step in firmly between them to let them know that they had better get back on the ball. But avoid the temptation to try to influence their feelings toward each other. No matter how much you'd like them to be more friendly, you probably won't succeed in changing their attitudes. You can only insist that their behavior toward each other doesn't hurt their effectiveness.

It's important to distinguish between behavior patterns that allow people to perform their immediate duties, and those that interfere with the duties of others. Your job in resolving personality conflicts between your subordinates is to make the person involved in the conflict aware how his or her behavior is adversely affecting others, and how it is thereby adversely affecting the operation.

Heading Off an Interdepartmental Feud

Managers faced with stories of how someone in another department creates obstacles, or with talk from another department that one of their own subordinates is uncooperative, should move immediately to head off further trouble. If they don't, the bad feeling can be contagious. As the trouble drags on, others get involved out of loyalty or sympathy.

Furthermore, the "hands-off" boss looks helpless or uninterested. Employees expect a manager to take action when they encounter obstacles to doing their jobs.

It's also possible that the manager's subordinate may be using the interdepartmental squabble to cover up his or her own deficiencies. "I can't do my job because of that so-and-so" may be his explanation, when in actuality he can't do his job—period.

If you are faced with interdepartmental friction, your first instinct may be to discuss the problem with the boss of the other subordinate. It's better, however, to start with some action on your own turf.

Try to find out the facts—yourself. What you have been getting is one person's emotional, self-serving interpretation. Simple observation, perhaps some offhand questions to other subordinates, may give a clearer picture of what is going on.

Discuss what should be rather than what is. Press your feuding subordinate to describe an alternative to the present problem. Chances are this will take some time because the subordinate's first reaction will probably be to blame the other person entirely. Make it clear that, at this stage, all you want is to know what would constitute cooperation in the subordinate's eyes.

Ask what the subordinate can do to help eliminate the bottlenecks and friction. Again, you may have to be persistent in putting the question, because in the employee's mind there is nothing he or she can do; the other person will have to change. Eventually you should be able to uncover certain areas in which your subordinate, by giving a bit, could work around the other's eccentricities and obstacles.

Once you've talked to your own subordinate, you are ready to discuss the problem with the manager of the other department, with or without both subordinates present. You and your subordinate are dealing from a position of strength, because you have taken the first steps toward creating a more cooperative atmosphere.

When the table is turned and another manager comes to you about the obstructive attitude of your subordinate, try to reserve judgment. Don't speak either out of automatic loyalty to the employee in your department or out of your own willingness to believe another manager. By agreeing something must be done and asking for a meeting at a later date, you give yourself time to take the steps described above before committing yourself or your subordinate to any action.

Holding on to Your Scalp in Others' Conflicts
You don't have to be directly involved in a conflict to get hurt. Imagine yourself in the following situation. Two managers are in competition for the job of executive vice president. The present holder retires shortly. Everybody knows it, and people are taking sides. Art, one of the two, asks you to lunch several times and solicits your advice more often then he used to do. Paul has always been rather stern, but even he seems warmer these days.

If you are like most managers, the intracompany struggle can be uncomfortable. You may find that people assume you are in one camp or the other, often for trivial reasons. If you attempt to remain outside the battle, you may be suspected by both sides. In the midst of all this, you still have to keep your day-to-day operations going. It is sometimes amazing that office politics can permeate so many activities with such intensity.

Regardless of the position you take in the conflict, you have to make sure your primary management responsibility is fulfilled.

Separate your job from the game-playing. You have certain tasks to do. Keep your own independent judgment active in performing these tasks. Concentrate, tough as it may be sometimes, on doing your job the way that you judge is right.

Avoid discussing the political situation with subordinates. You may be a manager who believes in maximum openness, but this should apply to the job, not to the infighting. Your secretary may have a natural curiosity about who's on top; your assistant may maintain that he can do his job better if he is privy to the latest inside dope. Close your ears to their pleas.

Remember the chain of command. Whatever your inclinations or bets on the outcome of the struggle, make sure you continue to fulfill your responsibilities to those currently in authority. Even if you feel you must commit yourself to one side or the other, you'll probably find it to your advantage not to do so quickly. Managers sometimes inject themselves into fights when they don't mean to, or don't have to.

Decide what's in your own self-interest. Perhaps you can't afford to stay put. Your survival (not to mention advancement) in the organization could depend on getting into the fray. On the other hand, you may feel that you couldn't look yourself in the mirror unless you intervene on the side you think is right. You're not thinking only of your job; but also of your conscience.

Ask what role you can play. It's possible that you could act as a mediator, as an easer of tension, in which case you must be trusted by both sides. However, don't let yourself be used as an informant or pipeline, passing information back and forth. If you do, people will tell you only what they want the other side to know.

Whatever you do, say the same thing to both sides. It's not easy to be honest and objective; nerves are raw, people are touchy. Nevertheless, avoid the temptation to tell people on each side what they want to hear. If you have opinions and feelings, lay them on the line when appropriate. You may be temporarily unpopular, but this is better than being considered devious and unreliable.

Prepare for the post-battle letdown. In a company fight, managers often find themselves being courted by the protagonists. This gives them a heady feeling, and they sometimes let themselves be carried away.

All battles end, however. One side wins, the other loses. Or, as frequently happens, a compromise is worked out, and the rift is papered over in a way that would have seemed impossible a few weeks before. The ranks close. When this happens, the manager who acts as if the battle were still going on will be making a major mistake. The manager may have been given unusual latitude during the fighting; this is likely to end. He or she may have enjoyed exceptional cordiality; this will cool a little. The manager may have been fed confidential data; the flow may stop.

Before the struggle is resolved, it is a good idea to anticipate its ending and to get ready for the changes (or the return to normal) that will take place when the truce is signed.

You'll need to exercise discretion after the armistice, too. Wounds may not heal quickly, even though people are smiling again. Be careful not to make unnecessary references to the recent conflict. That just opens the wounds.

chapter8 Countering Communications Problems

Few managers would say that criticizing a subordinate is easy. It's often painful for the manager doing the reprimanding. That's why executives sometimes resort to ways to ease the pain for themselves, such as the four ways listed below. As techniques they usually backfire, because their effect is not to encourage desired behavior change so much as to make an unpleasant job more bearable.

The sandwich technique. This approach involves a generous hunk of criticism between two thin slices of praise, as illustrated in an exchange between a firm's chief auditor and one of her traveling subordinates. The chief opened the conversation by complimenting the auditor on the latter's willingness to take on some of the tougher jobs, even though it meant being away from home for weeks at a time. "Just like our Northwest plants, for example. That kept you away for six weeks, and I know some of the towns aren't very exciting."

"Of course," she added, "six weeks is a long time. I can understand why toward the end you might have wanted to cut corners."

EMPLOYEE: What do you mean?

CHIEF: Well, your inventory figures for the Spo-
             kane plant are off—quite a bit, to be honest.
             You must have been taking other people's
             word for the inventory levels. And that's not
             our job. You should have checked it out
             yourself. Anyway, we've caught it now,
             luckily. Everything else seemed in order,
             like most of your work. You really break
             your back. I just wish some of the younger
             fellows around here would take a leaf out of
             your book."

In mixing praise with criticism, this manager risks diluting
the impact of both. The criticism seems to be an incidental
matter, when it is actually very important to the chief. What is
worse, the praise itself has been contaminated. The next time
this auditor hears his boss praise him, he'll be so busy
wondering what he did wrong and when the other shoe will
drop, that he won't hear or appreciate the good things the boss
is saying about him.

Sandbagging is another criticism technique to avoid. It has its
analogy in poker, when one person checks another into a
cinch. A player who feels strongly that he holds the winning
hand does not bet but rather checks, that is, passes without
betting. His aim is to lure another player into making a bet
that the checker can raise heavily. Most poker players frown
on this practice, and many outlaw it.

There are times when managers will check a subordinate
into a cinch. As illustration, here's an exchange between a sales
manager and a salesman.

"Jerry," says the manager, "about the Atarax account. Have
you followed up on their last problem? As I recall, they were
pretty hot under the collar."

"No need to worry. I took care of it."

"And you've gotten back to them to find out whether all the
bugs are out of the equipment now?"

"They're very happy," Jerry replies.

The manager reaches into a folder and pulls out a letter
from the Atarax president. "As you can see, it is addressed to

our president. It plainly says there has never been any follow-up on the initial service. And you can see they are not very happy at all!"

The salesman has been trapped. He won't forget this interview. The only problem is, he won't remember what he should—that he didn't tell the truth, that he hadn't really done his job. Rather, he'll remember resentfully that his boss sandbagged him.

It's one thing to hold the winning cards. It's another thing to play them in a way that humiliates another.

Firing a broadside is another form of ineffectual criticism; when this technique is used, everyone catches hell for what a few are doing. In a large insurance company that maintains an employee cafeteria, a department head notices that three of her supervisors (out of fourteen) frequently take more than the allotted hour for lunch. She writes a memo to be circulated to all supervisors that the one-hour lunch maximum is to be observed, and that taking longer will figure in the annual appraisal and salary review.

The evils in this shotgun approach are obvious. It unfairly condemns the innocent along with the guilty. The innocent are offended, while the guilty conclude that everyone else has been doing the same thing they have. Thus the guilty may feel they can continue committing the same offense.

This type of memo is a departure from sound management practice. The manager made no effort to analyze the problem, determine its causes, and develop a realistic solution. Her memo will get one result: a lot of her supervisors will be annoyed with her for a long time to come.

One of the most amusing instances of firing a broadside involved the president of a leading Manhattan advertising agency. He stepped into the elevator one morning and found himself standing next to a scruffy-looking fellow—long hair, beard, dirty, unconventional clothes. Furthermore, the chap smelled. To the executive's dismay, the young fellow got off the elevator at his floor and walked into the agency.

The president followed and demanded of the receptionist, "Does that man work for me?"

"Yes, sir, he's the art director on the XYZ account."

The president went into his office and wrestled with his conscience. Obviously the art director was good at his job; XYZ was one of their most contented accounts. Furthermore, a "creative" agency should not demand rigid conformity from its staff. But some things are just too much, the president decided, and dictated a memo to the art department staff announcing that each of them was required to bathe daily.

The advertising agency president was like many executives who find it embarrassing to talk to another individual about personal appearance or behavior. They resort to memos to avoid pointing the finger at a specific person, especially when the matter involves personal taste and possibly personal prejudice. Managers feel uneasy about that—justifiably. Conformity for the sake of conformity is not particularly popular in many circles today. To demand rigid conformity may create a backlash far more serious than the original offense.

There's another reason why a manager may resort to shotgun criticism. When a large number of people may be involved in breaking some rule or custom, it's often difficult to identify the guilty parties. Such a memo can therefore be construed as a form of laziness. Before committing criticism to paper, the wise manager will ask these questions:

Do I really have a sound, defensible reason for expressing this criticism?

Am I hiding behind paper because I shrink from a personal confrontation?

Is every person to whom it is directed equally guilty?

Will it actually achieve the desired change of behavior, or merely create hostility?

Is there a better way than the written word—individual conversations or group discussions, for example?

Playing psychoanalyst also undermines criticism. The would-be psychoanalyst doesn't merely tell someone what he did wrong; he tells him what kind of psychological motivation drove him to do it.

Here's a manager confronting an employee with his most recent example of failure to carry out instructions. "You know, Jack, it's not only this time. I've always sensed a—well, resentment on your part toward me. I guess you don't like the idea of a boss, of having to take orders. Maybe you have a father problem. You probably see me as a father figure, and you resent me for it."

Truthfully, whether Jack disliked his father and now transfers that resentment to his boss is not really the issue. If there has been a series of insubordinate acts, then the manager may be right that Jack has a problem, but what sort of problem is a decision that the boss should leave to a professional to diagnose and treat.

The above errors—sandwiching criticism between praise, sandbagging, firing a broadside, playing psychoanalyst—may seem to lessen the pain of giving criticism, but they can cause even greater problems. Furthermore, some of the benefits of constructive criticism—learning, recognition, measurement of performance—are lost. The following sections deal with these benefits and how to get them.

Describing What You've Seen

Perhaps the most important consideration in offering criticism is to confine yourself to a discussion of what the subordinate has done that you feel is offensive or counter-productive. That means talking about behavior, not psychology.

Many discussions involving appraisal of conduct or performance never get off the ground because people never agree on the description applied to the person being criticized. Everyone bridles at being labeled.

If you've ever fallen into the trap of describing someone as "insensitive," "defensive," or "abrasive," then you know how futile the use of such labels can be. They are your interpretations, open to question. Using them gives you a chance to let off steam, but usually nothing more. You can get much better results by limiting yourself to describing specific, observable acts.

You can call an employee irresponsible or you can say, "This job was to be finished by the 13th and it wasn't completed until the 15th." You may feel that an employee, in laughing at another's idea, is insensitive. But you'll get a better response from that person if you say, "When you laughed, I saw Don frown and look away. I think you may have offended him."

People are likely to be less defensive when presented with observed acts, something concrete to deal with, rather than personal interpretations. By describing the behavior you witnessed, you are less open to charges of prejudice, and there is a greater chance of achieving some resolution.

Learning from Criticism
Criticism is not only recognition, proof of the boss' concern, it can be a vital learning experience for both boss and subordinate.

There is general agreement among behavioral scientists that most people are turned on by learning on the job. Criticism can provide an occasion for growth and development, provided it is not the only thing subordinates hear from their boss. But it must be used thoughtfully if it is to serve as an incentive. In addition to confining discussion to the behavior observed or the performance measured, you may wish to follow these suggestions.

Criticism should follow the behavior as soon as possible. The experience is fresh in the mind of the subordinate. Rationalizations haven't had time to firm up, nor have anxieties been able to fester. If the employee knows something was done wrong, then he or she worries about what will happen. Relieving the tension as quickly as possible by recognizing the mistake is almost a kindness.

Get the subordinate's analysis of the situation first. Even though you may know more of the answers than the person who is being criticized, find ways to let the individual who made the mistake tell you what went wrong. Then ask how it can be avoided next time. The subordinate may not really accept your analysis. It's a different matter, though, with any improvements and safeguards the subordinate suggests. So emphasize the questions "What do you think went wrong?" and "How can we prevent this in the future?"

However, you must keep your objectives firmly in mind. The employee may be defensive, perhaps even antagonistic. He or she may ramble or go off on a tangent. You want the session to be a learning and improving experience; the employee may seek self-justification. Be considerate, but bring the discussion back to your own objectives. You may need patience. If possible, keep the session going until you feel you have accomplished what you intended and the employee agrees on the steps to be taken.

Concentrate on the lesson to be learned. What's the point of wasting a lot of time rehashing what will probably never come up again? Single out those aspects that may recur or mistakes that may be repeated in future situations and work with those. How can the problems be avoided? How can procedures or methods be overhauled? How can safeguards be established?

Expect the criticism to teach you something, too. You may not know all the facts, after all. For example, the employee may have encountered some problems with another department that you haven't heard about. Or a more senior employee may have interfered and changed procedures. Or the employee may have encountered some antiquated standard operating procedures that badly need changing. If you don't learn anything from the criticism session, you may have missed something helpful to you and to the operation. You may have just been giving your opinion, instead of showing that you recognize the value of the subordinate's work.

Mixing Criticism with Praise
As mentioned above, most management experts say that the sandwich technique—delivering criticism sandwiched be-

tween two layers of praise—is poor practice. The praise dilutes the criticism, and when the criticism does sink in, then the praise loses its value to the employee and may even sound manipulative. "You set me up for this, you..." is what the employee may wind up thinking.

Ideally, praise and criticism should be separated. Yet there are times when the whole message has to be delivered at once, the bad along with the good. It may be important for the subordinate to get the total picture of the project he or she is engaged in. Or perhaps this is the only chance you're going to have to talk with the person. Or the subordinate has to take some immediate remedial action in a matter that generally has turned out well except for one aspect.

At such times it's difficult and downright unrealistic for you to resolve to stick only to the good or the bad. How can you say all you have to say without blunting the impact of either the criticism or the praise? You can avoid the sandwich technique and make the effect you want if you:

Start with the negative by announcing that you are concerned with the minus side first. Discuss what's wrong without mixing in any praise.

Get agreement on the points under criticism. Does the employee understand what you are negative about? The relative seriousness of it?

Devise and get a commitment for remedial action, if such is required. "Okay, you'll have the revised figures to me no later than Wednesday?"

Once you've covered the less pleasant side, secured understanding, and agreed on plans for correction or future avoidance, go on to the positive.

Give the plus points their due, but in proportion to the minuses. You may be tempted to exaggerate some of the good features of the subordinate's work to ease the pain of the criticism you've just unloaded. But that's precisely why you're using this technique rather than the sandwich—to make sure the subordinate hears all you want to say. If the good side doesn't count for much, don't make it sound great. Acknowledge it and leave it at that. On the other hand, if the good far outweighs the bad, you might say, "I wanted to cover the negative points. There aren't that many, but they are important. Now that we have taken care of them, I want to tell you how very impressed I was on the whole."

Don't go back to the negative. You don't need to. You already have established an understanding of what is wrong and what should be done about it. You don't want to take the pleasure out of what is right.

Choosing the Phone over the Pen

"I've been informed that, in order to expedite delivery, you called Shipping directly to try to convince them to use a faster and more expensive carrier. I can understand your wish to please the new customer, but I have to remind you that what you did was against our established procedures. I think you'll agree with me that over the long haul these procedures must be observed by everyone."

A perfectly correct memo, but chances are, if you received it, you'd react negatively. The saleswoman who had finally obtained a very large order from a customer she had been working a year to land was furious.

The written word sometimes conveys coldness or even hostility, although that was not the author's intention. The fact that a manager may not be angry or hostile when he writes a memo is no guarantee that his words won't imply such a mood to the person receiving it.

The manager who is about to write a memo should stop to consider that the written word is:

Unilateral. It conveys no sense of mutual communication. The writer has spoken, but the recipient was not able to reply. The words are there on paper and cannot be changed.

Blind. The person who writes the memo cannot see the reaction of the one receiving it.

Tension-building. Time and distance form a barrier. Although the recipient might like to reply—to clarify, to correct—he or she cannot until some time has passed. And that is frustrating.

Indelible. When most people recall a conversation, they tend to remember only what they want to remember. Any unpleasant aspects are usually tempered or modified by the passage of time. In a written memo, however, all the words, pleasant and unpleasant, remain.

One-dimensional. In some Asian languages, a word or sound may have several meanings; the precise meaning is determined by the speaker's pitch and tone of voice. To a lesser degree, the same is true in English. Precise meaning is conveyed not only by the word itself, but also by the speaker's volume, expression, and pitch. But this is not true of the written word. The reader usually sees only one meaning. It may not be the author's.

A public record. A conversation is heard only by those within earshot. But a number of people may see what has been written. Where will the memo be filed? How accessible will it be?

It's not that the written word is wrong or that conveying a message in writing is always bad management practice. There are times when putting words on paper is clearly justified, even unavoidable. But it's a good thing for a manager to remember that the risks of misunderstanding are greater in writing.

A manager wanting to complain, to argue a controversial point, to criticize, or to set forth partisan views ought to review the above considerations. Instead of writing, he or she may then decide to pick up the phone.

Delivering the Bad News

When a manager delivers bad news to a subordinate is just as important as what the news is and how the boss puts it. Obviously the manager wants to prevent serious damage to the subordinate's work effectiveness and to help the employee deal with the news constructively. A few points about timing:

The bad news should not be conveyed just before the subordinate has to face a demanding challenge in his or her job. Even if the employee is able to do this successfully, the psychic wear and tear will take its toll.

Lunch is probably not a good time to unload bad news, especially if the disappointing development has serious consequences or is quite unexpected. The same applies to just before lunch. The employee can do a lot of disgruntled, resentful talking to fellow workers. The end of the day or the week might be a good time, if the subordinate needs a chance to think it over, to choose alternatives or to design corrective measures. If the message is just plain bad news, though, it's best not to send the individual away to brood about it at home.

In many cases the optimum time for criticism is early in the day. This allows the subordinate time to think it over, and also affords the opportunity for a second discussion that same day. The second discussion can be important in concentrating on plans for improvement, binding up the wounds, showing the subordinate that management's regard for him or her has not diminished. Even if there is no formal discussion, the manager's normal interactions with the employee later in the day will help to stabilize the situation and soothe the employee's bad feelings.

Of course, early in the day might not be best for an employee who gets a slow start on the day. If a person's energy curve is usually highest in the afternoon, that may well be the time when he or she can best cope with disappointment or frustration.

Sidestepping the Put-down of Another Person

Executives have to take special care to watch out for the implications of their remarks about others. Since they are privy to more information than others are, it's assumed they have the inside story—if there is one. And people in high stations like it to be known that their knowledge of the operations is complete, that they can give the whole picture. Unfortunately, even a completely factual statement can be misunderstood or misinterpreted. A statement that seems harmless to the executive can be blown all out of proportion by someone else. And when it's a remark that denigrates or puts someone else down, the aftermath can become more than a little embarrassing for everyone concerned.

For example, a field sales manager was assigned to his insurance company's eastern sales division. The company, which had recently purchased a regional insurer, had some specialized lines that the absorbed company had not offered. The smaller company's agents now looked forward to having expanded lines of insurance to sell. They were eager to get going with the new lines.

Working night and day, the field sales manager met that need. In doing so he made a great deal of money—for the company as well as for himself. When he was praised to a higher executive, the executive's sole reply was, "Yes, he's a good man. But there's no way he could not have been a success with what we gave him." The truth, nothing but the truth—but a put-down just the same. At least, that's the way it was interpreted by the eastern division manager when he heard about it. Much bad feeling resulted, and eventually the executive was forced to apologize to the field manager.

The comparison is another way of robbing a person of satisfaction. "He's great. But compared to . . ." or, "Yes, she's super. But you should have seen Mike when he was in peak shape." The takeaway—"Yes, but she couldn't have done it without the family money behind her"—is another.

Yet another way is to create mystery, to imply that what outsiders see is not all there is. Executives are especially vulnerable to this trap because of their greater knowledge. "Yes, it was a good decision. Fortunately we were able to talk him out of what he wanted to do." Anytime someone implies that what went on behind the curtain is quite different from the public view, a put-down may result.

No one likes it. The put-down stings the victim, makes the

audience squirm, and leaves the speaker trying to rationalize what was said. People who put things "in perspective" by lowering someone else's achievements may end up feeling they've lowered themselves.

There are times when you may justly feel that another person doesn't merit such fulsome praise. To avoid being insincere and yet not put someone down, stop and think before you reply. Can't you let it go with a vague but positive "Yes, he's a good man"? Or, at most, "She's the kind of person we like to put all our chips on."

Does your audience *need* to know that there is a negative or less attractive side? If not, what will you be conveying? Could you come out of it diminished in your audience's eyes?

Choosing the Place to Talk to Subordinates

Often an executive's conversations with employees take place in the executive's office. But there are times when it is wise to reverse the process. You may get better results by dropping in on a subordinate in the following circumstances:

You want to clear the air. You may have had to criticize or reprimand someone on your staff. It's a good idea, a while later, to stop by and chat with that person about another matter. This shows everyone that things are back to normal. You are not holding a grudge and you do not expect the subordinate to harbor ill feeling.

Similarly, it may be common knowledge that an individual is dejected because of being passed over for a promotion or failing badly on some project. Stopping to chat with the person is a sign that you still consider the subordinate a valuable member of the team. This should enhance the person's feelings of self-worth and help him or her to recover from the disappointment and bounce back to normal more quickly.

You suspect someone has a problem. Occasionally subordinates get into situations (at times beyond their control) where they really need help, but are reluctant to ask for it. They may feel they must solve any problem themselves.

When you get an inkling of this kind of trouble, you make the idea of talking about it less forbidding if you drop in on the person concerned. Even if your subordinate doesn't raise the problem, you can lay the groundwork for a frank but comfortable discussion in the near future.

Perhaps you know the other person is long-winded. Despite your chat-is-over signals, you may have problems getting a long-winded subordinate out of your office. Talking in that person's territory may be a time-saver since, as the visitor, you can more easily end a conversation.

You have a new employee. New staff members are usually self-conscious or reluctant to see the boss about a problem or even to bring up a question. Going to see them in the early weeks builds a communication bridge between you and suggests that you welcome the same behavior.

You want to lessen the sting. No one relishes hearing about mistakes. Talking it out in the subordinate's office is more informal, shows it's not the end of the world, thus reducing the pain.

You want to talk privately without closing the door. A closed door tells others that a private conversation is taking place, and often sets them speculating as to what it's all about. Many executives find they can talk privately in the subordinate's office without having to close the door and reveal that "something is going on." There is usually less passing traffic in the subordinate's office and there are likely to be fewer interruptions.

You don't have the records but your subordinate does. If your discussion is going to center on figures or records in the employee's file or desk, it saves time for both of you to talk in your subordinate's area.

Encouraging without Promising

A manager, in conveying expectations that the employee will do well, may convey more than is advisable. For example, one executive, talking to a subordinate who is about to take on a demanding assignment, says, "Lou, I have every confidence in your ability. And we need people with that kind of ability. You know that we've been talking for some time about opening up a new division within the year. If you can handle this project the way I think you can, I don't see any reason why you won't have a very important part in the building of that division."

When the new division is finally set up, a candidate from outside the company is brought in to head it up. Lou angrily presents himself in the manager's office to say, "Six months ago, here in this office, you promised me that I'd head up that operation."

The boss protests, sincerely, that he had done no such thing. But nothing he says can mollify the employee. As the latter sees it, a specific promise was made and broken.

Such a "promise" is often made after a manager has been somewhat critical of a valued subordinate—this is one of the moments when the temptation is strongest—or as in the above case, when a manager is trying to persuade a subordinate to take on a tough or unpleasant assignment. Other occasions when inadvertent "promises" are made are when a manager is trying to help a good employee out of a temporary slump, or when a manager is anxious to recruit a top-notch person. In each case it is natural to want to paint a rosy picture of the future, and to put in some specifics to make that picture believable.

One of the most common mistakes people make in communicating with each other is to assume that, because we have heard ourselves say something, the other person has heard it too and, moreover, has heard exactly what we heard ourselves say. There is *always* the possibility of misunderstanding, that our statements will sound different to someone else than they do to us.

How can the problem be avoided? Obviously it isn't taboo for a manager to indicate that good work will have its rewards. But the mistake that the above manager made—and that many executives make—is to talk in specific terms. His reference to the new division, in the employee's mind, sounded like a commitment.

When you're holding up a promising vista of the future before the eyes of a subordinate, consider these suggestions:

Leave out the dates, facts, and figures. They may come back to haunt you.

Think about what you're saying as if you were putting it down on paper.

Try to hear it from the subordinate's point of view. What is the most favorable possible construction he or she could put on your words?

Translate the future into a challenge. "This is a growing organization. There will be more than enough tough jobs for the person who shows ability to handle them."

Giving the Right Impression in an Interview

An especially critical situation is the interview. Considering someone for a job requires skillful communicating on your part.

These days there are lots of qualified people out there competing for almost any job, true. But you would like the best. And the best are very likely people who know their own worth. They can be turned off quickly if the people who interview them give the wrong impression.

Consider one vice president who was very pleased about his interview with a young man he thought perfect for the product manager's position. The vice president thought they'd established a really close rapport. He was most unpleasantly surprised when, soon after, the applicant said "No, thanks."

"It was just one of those great interviews," recounted the vice president. "I saw him immediately as part of our team. He fit. He didn't give any indication that he wasn't interested.

Yet when I called him back a week later, after I'd gotten an okay on salary, I found he'd taken another job."

The applicant's side of the story was quite different. "I flew from Chicago to Nashville on short notice because they were so eager to see me. From then on it was all downhill. He told me about his record with the company, how much they had grown, the tremendous plans they had in the works. For over an hour he did most of the talking, but when I walked out I still didn't know anything about the job. And I didn't think he knew much about me. I had to assume he wasn't interested enough to find out."

When a candidate has heard only about the executive, the others in the operation, and the past accomplishments of the organization, and nothing about the specific job and its requirements, he or she can easily walk out of the interview thinking, "I don't think they know what they want. Certainly they don't seem enthusiastic about me."

Describe the company's operation. Executive interviewers often overestimate the amount of homework an applicant will do on the organization. In fact, the better known the company, the less research job seekers may do. Don't assume the applicants know all about your organization. Make a list of the vital facts about the organization so that the candidate can understand the context of the specific job that is open.

Make a list of the job requirements. Be sure the candidate understands the features and functions of the job itself. Keep both lists in front of you during the interview. You don't have a good prospect until you know that the job looks appealing to the applicant. A job is unlikely to look appealing unless the applicant knows what kind of a job it is, and in what kind of organization and environment.

Be careful with "problem" questions. A third pitfall to avoid is seeming to ask for unpaid work. An executive will ask candidates, "We have this problem. How would you solve it?" This can be a legitimate question. But it sometimes is posed in a way that suggests the executive is looking for a free consultation. If the candidate feels used, the organization may get neither consultation nor applicant. A way of posing the question that does not suggest exploitation might be, "Have you ever had this kind of problem in your previous employment? If so, how did you handle it?" Show that it's the applicant you want to know about, that you're not looking for free advice.

Using Stress in Interviews

Another factor in interviewing may color you, in the applicant's mind, as not a good person to work for. That's the use of stress.

Should you test job applicants and candidates for promotion by using stress interviews? A lot of managers like the idea. They are worried about the increasing cost of hiring and training people for responsible positions. They want to be as sure as possible that some hidden flaw won't emerge later on.

Then, too, many contemporary executives have studied some psychology. They know a number of testing techniques. They are interested in applying them on the job wherever they seem relevant. And it's only logical they should want to see how the applicant for a difficult post stands up under pressure when there is no way of observing the individual in a real-life work situation.

So they create stress. One way is to greet the candidate at the office door with a smile, conduct the person to a chair, then sit down behind the desk and stare—silently. The idea is that the job prospect will "break" and blurt out information that would remain hidden in the usual polite give-and-take. Of course, the manner of someone subjected to the silent treatment can be revealing, too.

Another approach is to ask blunt, personal questions. "Do you always dress that way?" "Why do you keep taking your glasses off?" "Why are you acting so defensively?" (This last is sometimes used even when the person is behaving in a poised and open manner.)

A more common technique is to encourage interruptions,

have a secretary enter the office two or three times, take all phone calls, invite associates to come in for consultations. The applicant may find it more and more difficult to maintain a sense of continuity and confidence. The "real" person will gradually emerge under pressure—or so the theory goes. Of course, this theory suggests that only negative behavior is "real."

One unintended consequence of the stress interview is that you can lose a well-qualified person. The prospect may walk out of the session saying, "Why should I work with someone who gives me such a bad time?"

Another is that the pressure created may not remotely resemble that experienced on the job. How the candidate behaves in this artificial situation is, then, irrelevant and the whole interview pretty much a waste of time.

A job interview is in itself a stress situation for the candidate. If you are interested in applying more pressure, keep these recommendations in mind:

Use stress only for a stress job. Only if applicants would frequently be under unusual pressure should you consider putting them under unnecessary stress ahead of time. For example, a manager who will take on an entirely new venture or a project that involves sophisticated technology may run into repeated, unexpected problems from all quarters. An executive who is being put in charge of an operation that is in deep trouble financially will be under constant fire. These are cases where stress interview techniques may be justified, if the conditions of the interview can be created to resemble somewhat those of the job.

Use a professional. If you feel that a stress interview is necessary, engage the services of a reputable professional who is thoroughly experienced in creating stress and handling its consequences.

Occasionally an executive who tries to use stress finds that the candidate has little tolerance for it and may actually have a brief breakdown in the office. That's not the kind of situation most executives are prepared to deal with.

There is also a less dramatic reason for using a professional. The candidate, if hired, won't have to work with the individual who put the pressure on. There is no residue of resentment, as there will very likely be if you create the stress.

Avoiding Embarrassment in Announcing a Termination

Going to the other end of the spectrum, managers are often tempted to cover up the real reason why an employee who has been fired is leaving. Here's a memo that probably has a familiar ring.

"We are sorry to announce that Steve Palchuk will soon be leaving us. He is presently negotiating a very attractive new job elsewhere, and he feels it is an opportunity that he cannot afford to turn down. We wish him the very best in his new career, and express our appreciation for the fine job he did here." Such a memo is well intentioned, of course, but it will not prevent Steve Palchuk from leaving under a cloud.

Of course, it might be argued that the best way to avoid embarrassment, credibility gaps, and cover-ups that get exposed is simply to tell the truth. This is something that has to be determined by the manager and the employee in question. Much will depend on the nature of the work, the causes of the failure, the organizational climate, and the personalities involved.

When making this type of decision, a manager should take at least two things into consideration. First, there will always be those who suspect that the reason for a cover-up is to protect the manager from the charge that he or she made a mistake in hiring. Second, in promulgating a cover story, the manager may compel others to become unwilling accomplices in spreading untruth. The resentment this can arouse may become an ongoing problem. In many cases, therefore, the truth may be the simplest and best way out of the situation.

If you want to cover up, agree to do so from the outset. Decide on your strategy and begin to put it into effect before the rumors get started. It may not be easy to find a plausible story, one you can stick to for the period of time required, but explanations that are born in haste are usually subject to revision and soon lose all credibility.

In making an announcement, try to avoid raising questions you can't answer. The mention of the "very attractive new job" that Steve Palchuk was supposedly negotiating would be bound to spur curiosity. Naturally, people would ask questions about it—questions that could cause embarrassment if there really were no such job. Some might also offer congratulations, causing even more embarrassment.

Let people know what their relationship with the soon-to-be-terminated employee will be. Undoubtedly, people will ask whether they should continue to work with him on the same basis until he leaves. Or have his responsibilities changed? Clue them in, therefore, to the realities of the job situation. In some cases you may want to spell out which duties the outgoing employee will keep in the interim, and which ones are to be immediately transferred to others.

Some managers feel that in situations of this kind the best way to avoid a continuing strain is to isolate the on-the-way-out employee officially. He is relieved of any liaison work with others, not required to attend departmental meetings or submit weekly reports, and so on.

Try to resist the temptation to praise excessively the person who is leaving. If the employee has been around for some time, chances are that people know the kind of work he or she has done and whether it merits real praise. If it doesn't, then words of false praise will only create a credibility problem. Similarly, don't describe the employee's relationship with you and/or others as close and warm if it has been anything but that.

Making Noise about You

Many executives aren't sure how to publicize their own performance records. One way is to let the accomplishment speak for itself whenever possible. A design engineer, for example, keeps models of his best products on a table in his office. A plant manager keeps a large bulletin board of safety records and attendance figures.

Just spread the facts. If your accomplishment is less visible, it's okay to tell people what you have done. "We are 20% ahead of last year in government sales." But stick to the facts, and let people draw their own conclusions as to the value of the accomplishment and how much you are responsible for it.

When other people praise you in writing there is no reason why you can't post the congratulations publicly. But if you're praised orally, don't fall into the "Joe Smith told me that my project was the best he'd seen in years" trap. That sounds like bragging, and lessens the value of your accomplishment in the eyes of others.

Another way of calling attention to yourself is through the performance record of subordinates, or through proposing more challenge for your work group.

Call attention to the actual achievements of employees, not their potential. It's one thing to say, "My new supervisor, Fred Wynne, is going to do a better job in packaging and shipping than anyone I've ever had in there." It's quite another to be able to report to one's boss, "Three months in the job and Fred Wynne has those people shipping 22% more per day than ever before. Nobody ever got those people to work so well." If you picked Fred for the job, so much more credit for you.

Go after recognition for your employees. A lot of it will rub off on you. How about an article in the house organ? How about a request for a special salary increase for a superior performer? It calls attention to both of you. An innovative memo from a subordinate to you can be sent on with your comments. Good thinking in your department has to be partly a consequence of the climate you create.

Volunteer your department for more work, and a chance for more achievement. A tough job up? Grab it.

Just in case the message doesn't get across, and even if it does, here's solid advice: periodically make your bosses aware of your aspirations. The executive vice president is not omniscient, after all, and may well equate your satisfaction at doing a good job with a desire to stay put. When someone has a good record as a profit-maker, management is often leery of moving that person, particularly if he or she seems content to remain in the present job. Upward mobility hinges in part on letting others know what you are doing and what you can do, as well as what you want to do. Recognition has to be pursued.

Planning a More Effective Presentation

Enthusiasm is a fine quality, but it can get you into all sorts of difficulties when you are about to make a presentation or a report about something you are deeply involved in, committed to, or familiar with.

For example, because you are steeped in your subject, you may assume that your listeners are equally familiar with it. So you jump from point to point without realizing that at least some of your audience will not be able to make the connections, to complete the logical development. Or you may go to the other extreme and dwell so extensively on the details that your audience loses sight of the main point. You may try to cram too much substance into too little time. In trying to cover everything about the subject, you wind up telling the audience more than they need or want to know.

Either of these approaches can mean that you lose your audience to confusion or boredom, that you won't get the kind of reaction you hope for. It's very important to have some way of knowing how a presentation will sound to others.

No matter how simple or clear you think your presentation is, your chances for attention and comprehension will be increased substantially if you operate from the following assumptions.

Very likely there will be at least one person in the group who does not understand what you are saying.

Very likely no one in the group will know as much about the subject as you do (otherwise why are you giving the presentation?).

Very likely some people in the group think more slowly

than you do, and so will need more time to grasp what you are saying.

There are also other things you can do to make sure your presentation is a success.

Circle technical terms. Go through your notes and single out every word or phrase that is used in a technical sense. Be sure that each such term is defined the first time it is used, and that a recap of the definition appears the second time it is used. When several such terms are used close together, you may want to distinguish between them by repeated short definitions.

Make a visual. Supplementing your presentation with a visual is not as easy as it sounds. Many visual aids actually detract from a verbal presentation by being dull or repetitious, or by emphasizing too many minor points. Don't make your aids too wordy; that's not what visuals are for. Make them as graphic and nonverbal as possible, using them to underscore the difficult and important parts of your story.

Rehearse your presentation before someone who doesn't know the subject matter. Perhaps a colleague will be willing to give up some of his time, or you might ask your spouse to listen. Just be sure that your audience-of-one is advised to stop you at any point that he or she finds confusing.

Ask someone who will be in the group to act as a barometer. Get this person to agree to signal you when you move too rapidly over a point that is difficult to understand. If you get such a signal during your presentation, stop and ask whether everyone is following you.

Encourage questions. It sometimes seems more convenient to ask people to hold their questions until the end of the presentation. But that's a poor time to find out that you lost some—or even all—of your audience way back when. If a question is premature, make a note of it and promise to get back to it at a later time. If a question seems irrelevant or distracting, again make a note of it and deal with it at the end of your presentation. However, answer questions that are proper and to the point as they come up.

Provide follow-up. No matter how clearly you have presented your subject, people may want to know more about it after they have had a chance to think over your presentation. Perhaps they were distracted and missed some critical point in your talk. Or they may have been so busy assimilating the information you were providing that they didn't think of questions.

If the subject was important enough to warrant a presentation, it certainly deserves some follow-up time. This can be formal or informal: another meeting, for example, or simply an hour or two when you will be available to anyone who comes to you with questions or comments. This gives your audience a second chance to get the message. It also provides an opportunity for you to see how much of what you said was understood.

chapter 9 Making Meetings More Productive

Many otherwise successful executives run poor, ineffective meetings. Some of them fail—usually without realizing it—because their style of conducting a meeting runs to one of two extremes.

Some executives lean over backward to be democratic. They state the objectives of the meeting, then relinquish control—not necessarily in words but through their actions (or lack of them). The meeting may then stretch on interminably, ending with a compromise that results from fatigue or desperation rather than rational adjustment. Probably the most unfortunate result is that much of the knowledge, experience, and analytical ability of the group will be untapped—not to mention that personality conflicts may erupt as others struggle to fill the vacuum the leader has created.

Others keep the discussion firmly on a predetermined track to reach a predetermined objective in a predetermined period of time. This approach is often effective in insuring that the group achieves an immediate objective. However, the leader is likely to stifle suggestions for a better way to get the job done. Again, the group's resources will probably not be fully taken into account and utilized. Furthermore, autocratic or manipulative methods make it unlikely that everyone around the table will be committed to the goal the leader has decided upon. The result may be a lasting resentment that undermines the success not only of the present project but of future group efforts.

Effective meeting leaders know that there are certain formal functions they must undertake. For example, they should not only state the meeting's goal clearly at the start but also return to it from time to time, bringing people back to the subject if discussion becomes irrelevant.

One of the most critical leadership functions is to help develop alternatives. Groups often tend to select one solution early in the discussion and ride with it. It is up to the leader to be sure no possible alternative is being neglected because some participants hesitate to disagree with what's gone before.

A competent meeting leader also knows when to sum things up. Summarizing too early may forestall further helpful comments. On the other hand, waiting too long increases the likelihood that the discussion will already have become unfocused.

The final moments of a meeting can be vitally important to the action that should follow. The group must understand the significance of the solution chosen—how it relates to larger goals, its possible direct and indirect consequences. Before breaking up the meeting, the leader should get a commitment from each member to carry out any assigned responsibilities in the way the group has decided.

This chapter will elaborate on some of these leadership roles.

Choosing the Right Size

There is growing evidence that the most creative problem-solving or decision-making occurs in small, odd-numbered groups of five, seven, or nine people. Perhaps because a majority is possible, such groups seem to be more relaxed and efficient. Without fear of stalemate, people seem more likely to say what they think, even if there is disagreement. Five people is the number many researchers suggest for optimum efficiency, freedom of exchange, and cooperation.

In even-numbered groups, say four or six, there are more disagreements and fewer suggestions. There need not be unanimity for a decision to be reached (as in a group of two), but there is the possibility that they will split evenly. Participants in such groups tend to be aggressive in pushing their ideas.

As the group gets larger, the chance for individual participation becomes smaller. As a result, the most prevalent effect on individuals attending large meetings is frustration. If they come up with hot ideas, pertinent comments, or strong opinions, often they aren't able to voice these right away. It's annoying to think of a snappy response and then have to wait five minutes until you can deliver it.

People in large meetings compensate by offering fewer opinions but more information. Thus, the large group can be used more effectively to collect and disseminate information. The leader must exercise considerable control and direction.

Getting Ideas on the Table

"As you all know," the memo read, "we are taking a price beating on the West Coast. Local suppliers there are underselling us. We've scheduled a meeting tomorrow morning at 10:00 to try to hammer out a solution to the problem of how to get our products out there at a competitive price."

You may have received memos like this one. There are at least two reasons why the solution produced at the forthcoming meeting will not be as good as it could be.

The first impediment is created by the way the problem is defined. While those who will attend the meeting should be alerted to the general nature of the problem beforehand, managers may unwittingly define the problem in a way that limits the area of speculation. In the case mentioned above, the nature of the problem is: How can we be more effective or profitable in our West Coast selling? The wording of the memo restricts a solution to retaining manufacturing facilities on the East Coast, when conceivably a new West Coast facility or licensee might be the answer.

The second defect in the memo is that no one is asked to try to come up with a solution before the meeting.

The argument frequently made to the effect that a group generates more solutions than an individual is not necessarily borne out by research.

If you are planning a meeting to try to solve a problem, consider these three steps to help you get more ideas for the group to deliberate.

Don't define the problem as you see it. Describe the symptoms, or the consequences of continuing things as they are. Of course, if there are limits to the kinds of possible solutions, let the group members know in advance so they don't waste their time. For example, in the memo quoted above, the manager might have added, "Building a manufacturing facility of our own on the West Coast can't be considered. We just don't have the money at this time." Although the qualification restricts the possible range of answers, there is still a lot of room for people to work in.

Idea generation in a meeting is usually improved if you set aside time to write the answers presented on a blackboard or chart. Each person at the meeting describes his proposed solution, which is added to the list. (You may wish to limit the time for each description.)

There may be times when you'll be pleasantly surprised to find others in the group defining the problem quite differently from the way you have defined it. For example, in the case cited, one member says it is not primarily a price problem but a superior service feature that is not being exploited in sales interviews with prospects.

Ask members of the group not to debate or comment on the ideas while the proposed solutions are being recorded. The person who presents the idea is not allowed to argue for its acceptance, and no one else in the room is permitted to support it or criticize it. Questions to clarify points may be asked, but only when everyone has had a say is discussion permitted. This makes it easier for members of the group to really see and listen to what is presented. They don't have to formulate their opinions now. At this point the only thing expected of them is to understand what each member is contributing.

This technique, of course, does not guarantee that the best solution will be selected by the group. It does, however, assure that as many proposed solutions as possible get on record before partisanship is expressed. Furthermore, all ideas get an equal presentation.

Developing a Good Discussion

When the ideas are evaluated, dissociate them from the people who propose them. Try these tactics:

Discuss the idea with the group rather than with the originator. If people question or criticize an idea, suggest they present their queries or objections to the group as a whole instead of on a one-to-one basis with the person who offered it. If the originator wants to contribute to the discussion, fine, but he or she won't feel compelled to if not addressed personally.

Rephrase criticism in a positive way. If one person comments, "We tried that approach before and it didn't work because no one would use it," this might be paraphrased as, "What you're saying then, Liz, is that we would need understanding and support from other units if this is going to work."

You have to be especially watchful for the tendency of people in groups to settle on a solution as quickly as possible. They become impatient if anyone tries to examine the issue in detail. There are several reasons. First, some people may already have brought their pet solution with them, and in order to get it adopted they squelch any questioning. Other participants may feel uncomfortable with an unresolved situation, and will try to settle it as quickly as possible even at the risk of accepting a poor solution. Too, there is a tendency in groups to see situations in black and white, either-or. Some participants put on pressure to select a decision rather than prolong discussion. In such a situation, a group may find itself agreeing to a decision that most members haven't had a chance to think through.

If you feel your group is jumping to a decision which hasn't been properly thought out, you can take the following steps to prolong the deliberation.

Insist on taking time to state as many points as possible. Introduce some of the ideas that have not, in your judgment, been adequately considered. If you are sufficiently firm you may slow up action. You may arouse impatience or opposition from some of the participants, but this may be less risky than going along with a bad decision. You may need to say, "I'm not getting across how seriously I feel we ought to look at as many alternatives as possible. Does anybody else share my concern?" Or, "Does anyone else wonder, as I do, whether we're rushing into what could be a decision we'll have to undo?" Such an appeal for help can sometimes encourage others who have doubts to express them.

Refuse to agree to the proposed solution. It's a last resort, but it is available to you as leader. If you're not satisfied, say you can't vote on or approve the solution. One suggestion is to recess the meeting to give people more time to think.

It takes time to develop and explore options, to let the non-logical and unconscious processes work, to recognize and minimize whatever obstructive or prejudicial emotions affect you.

Too often, decisiveness—the tendency to make firm decisions fast—is mistakenly admired over careful decision-making, which can be a time-consuming, deliberate, detailed, and not always definable series of steps.

Making the Decision Stay Decided
One reason why you want to be sure of an adequate discussion

is that otherwise the decision, once made, may come undone. For example, your group has spent much time over the past two weeks evaluating the new miniature dictating equipment for your department. After having listened to salespeople, pored over technical material, and tried various equipment, you've made your choice—the Belden.

The next day, while you are polishing your recommendation to the boss that the department invest in Belden equipment, one of your group associates startles you by saying, "You know, I think we ought to run over this again. I know Belden is good, but maybe the Thomas would really be a better buy."

Inwardly, you begin to seethe at the thought of reopening the deliberations. The temptation is strong to argue against renewing the discussion or to say flatly, "Don't worry about it, we've made the right decision," and press ahead with the discussion of when the Belden should be installed. Neither approach will subdue your associate's feeling of conflict. For he is undergoing a phenomenon known as "cognitive dissonance." Either he is having second thoughts about the decision or he went along with the group without really being convinced.

As psychologist Leon Festinger notes in his book *Conflict, Decision and Dissonance,* ". . . the greater the conflict before the decision, the greater the dissonance afterward." When someone can't turn off the second thoughts and uneasiness, Festinger warns that "there may be considerable time during which the person continues to focus on dissonance without being able to reduce it materially." Such people may need substantial, specific help in getting rid of the discord and accepting the decision.

It takes patience to deal with people whose cognitive dissonance makes it difficult for them to act on a decision. But since they aren't likely to commit themselves to effective action while they're still mulling over the pros and cons, the effort is worthwhile. Some suggestions on how to proceed:

Anticipate continuing conflict. If reaching a decision involves much conflict, be ready for cognitive dissonance after the decision has been made. You might delay the actual decision-making until you get people's feelings about the alternatives, especially if there are signs that someone is pushing one course of action for emotional reasons.

Be prepared to listen. People who question a decision may simply want an opportunity to talk about their concern. You may not have to sell them on the rightness of the original decision; skillful and sympathetic questions can help them complete their thinking. That way you can convey reassurance and encourage them to live happily with what has been decided.

Have facts at hand to reinforce the decision. Anecdotes involving the success of others who have gone this route (or the failure of those who have not), statistics, a look ahead at the consequences of this approach—all of these can help doubters put their fears to rest.

Make it clear that you are open to reconsideration. Very often during the decision-making phase the idea gets across that once the choice has been made it will have to stick. Not surprisingly, this discourages people from bringing up later doubts openly. However, it doesn't discourage covert questions about the wisdom of the choice. And there could be a reluctance to implement the decision.

There may, after all, be sound reasons why the decision should be reconsidered. To create a supportive climate for questioning group decisions and for initiating post-mortems, one manager successfully introduced the following technique. He asks each participant to fill out a form a few days after the final session. Sample questions:

How confident did you feel at the end of the meeting about the correctness of the decision?

How confident do you now feel about the correctness of the decision? (Answers to both questions are marked on a scale of 1% to 100%.)

If you feel substantially less confident now, what factors have influenced you? (Or, what aspects of the decision would you like to see reviewed?)

In case of a disparity, the manager talks with the

respondent or suggests that he or she talk with others who participated in the decision. After the talk, the manager decides whether to resume deliberations with the group.

Today there is a growing belief that a decision arrived at by consensus is usually a better decision than one made individually or by majority vote. Because everyone has had an opportunity to express views and to evaluate extensively the contributions made, they are more likely to feel a sense of commitment. They haven't just gone along; they have built the decision. It is theirs.

Using a Group Effectively

Your leadership of a successful group will be remembered for some time. It's an unparallelled opportunity to get visibility and to create needed change.

If the group goes sour, however, it can set an ambitious manager back. One manager—we'll call him Fred—seemed the ideal choice to head up the task force that was being appointed to revamp his organization's distribution system. An engineer with a marketing MBA, he was bright, genial, and ambitious. He had demonstrated an impressive grasp of the dynamics and needs of the organization. His enthusiasm for the task force's project was clearly shared by the other managers and specialists serving on it.

Yet four months after the task force began meeting, no decisive steps had been taken. Progress was stymied. What's more, three of the seven members of the group had asked to be relieved of the assignment. Another attended meetings but refused to participate. Six out of the seven members reported that Fred was the primary reason for the team's failure. In their words, he was "impossible to work with."

It often happens, when a task force goes sour, that the group's leader gets the blame. In Fred's case, the other members charged that he ran the group with an iron fist, he made the members feel like rubber stamps, he hogged the spotlight, he made decisions in the group's name without involving the other members, and he generally seemed more interested in personal glory than in getting the job done.

Unfortunately Fred was totally unaware that his colleagues saw him this way. He paid little attention to the needs and feelings of the people associated with him.

Perhaps the most frequent reason why group leaders are misunderstood by other members is that they misunderstand their own roles.

For example, team-building should be their first concern. But they must often build where they will never be more than first among equals. Thus the group leader is wise to realize from the start that it will be dangerously easy to get out of step with "the troops"—because in this case "the troops" have no intention of marching to the manager's tune, if he is not their boss. They will be quick to resent any behavior that even appears to give the impression they are somehow under the leader.

What can you do to avoid getting into such a position? Very often a failure can be prevented if you will take the following precautions.

Work with everyone. You will probably encounter one or two members with whom you can work exceptionally well. Unfortunately, this may lead to the exclusion of other members. The manager who lets the group split into "ins" and "outs" will find that his or her effectiveness is diminished. The people who are left out will resent their exclusion. They may even, before they are through, sabotage everything the "in" members think they have accomplished.

Another potentially divisive situation is created when one member, who likes to operate behind the scenes, begins to consult you in private. No matter how valuable the ideas that emerge, you have to make sure that nothing is agreed to or done without the task force as a whole having a chance to discuss the plans. There is a fine line between getting everyone into the act all the time, which makes for unwieldiness, and leaving them offstage completely.

Keep the group informed of your outside contacts. The role of a task-force leader is to maintain liaison with others outside the group, and especially with top management, but this can be overdone. If the leader undertakes to report all the group's actions or deliberations to outsiders and then relay back all decisions that affect the group, that's almost a surefire formula to generate suspicion. Some members will believe they aren't in on the real action. Some will suspect they are hearing only what the leader chooses to tell them.

To counteract any left-out feelings, especially the suspicion that agreements are being secretly arrived at, the leader can occasionally invite the outside people with whom he consults to meet with the whole group. Getting the group's approval of whatever he or she communicates to outsiders also helps.

Keep time demands reasonable. It's a wise leader who bears in mind that task-force members have other responsibilities. Too frequent or too extensive meetings put them on the spot in their own departments.

This doesn't mean running a meeting so tightly that everyone feels unimportant and manipulated, but it does mean that occasionally someone may be frustrated because he or she didn't get to participate in every session as fully as that person would have liked.

Where possible, agree to limit the time of the meetings in advance. "Do you think we can get this done by noon?" or "Do you think we can cover this in an hour and a half?" Keep to the adjournment time whenever possible.

Let everyone share the glory. If you put out a communiqué, it's a good idea to put everyone's name on it. If you give an oral presentation, you can make sure everyone on the committee is identified. If possible, break up an oral presentation so that others have a chance to shine, or let them individually put out memos in the name of the group.

Let them have an identifiable piece of action. Having members of the group assume responsibility for specific segments or phases of the project is one way to get greater involvement. When people own part of the action, something that they can identify with and be recognized for, it helps to build cohesiveness in the long run. If the group is involved in a long-term project, asking other members to assume the chair on occasion—especially when their specialties or parts of the project are under discussion—gives the clear impression you are not out to steal the show.

Shutting People Off

You don't want to appear as sole judge of what is important. There are subtle ways in which you as chairman may prevent people from giving you their best in your meetings. Usually one is not conscious of the actions that are interpreted as judgmental or even as put-downs. For example:

Facial expression. One executive I know makes it obvious when he disagrees with what is being said. He flashes a look that seems to say, "How can anyone believe such nonsense?"

It's one thing for peers to reflect such feelings and thoughts in their faces. But when the boss does it, people start weighing their words extra carefully. Some very good words might go unsaid.

A show of impatience. Another executive has a low tolerance for what she considers rambling. She begins to shuffle papers, fidget, and glance at her watch. The message thus communicated is, "This fellow is not saying anything worth listening to, and I wish he'd finish in a hurry." The result is that no one bothers to pick a salient thought from what is said. The minute the fidgeting starts, others around the table assume very blank faces.

Another way people show impatience is to change the subject immediately after someone has spoken. Especially when the leader does this, the communication is, "Forget what was just said. It doesn't count."

Talking through. Interrupting and starting to speak before the other person has really finished are common. People get carried away with a thought. It suddenly seems so much more important than whatever is being said, and sometimes it is. But the person interrupted may feel put down. When it is the leader or boss who breaks in, the message conveyed is, "Don't bother with her. What she has to say isn't of any value. Listen to me."

Similarly, when the boss makes *sotto voce* comments to the person sitting in the next seat, others in the group will turn their attention to these comments rather than to the person who holds the floor.

Getting Results from a Committee You Appoint

What about the groups or committees you appoint but do not lead in person? Many executives consider committees a waste of time and effort. Yet the success or failure of a committee often depends upon the executive who appoints it.

Don't use the committee as a stamp. If you know in advance what you plan to do, never put a group through an exercise in order to put a team stamp on your decision. Your credibility will suffer, and the next committee you name will suspect at the outset that its deliberations are a waste of time. You won't get anything worthwhile out of the members, even if you honestly want them to come up with fresh ideas.

Accept indecision. If a committee cannot arrive at a decision or even a recommendation, accept the lack of decision rather than forcing it to come up with something, no matter what. This will never make you look bad. In fact, it shows your good sense in exploring all possibilities before you make the final decision on a tough problem.

Let the members decide on their own leader. Even managers who have the good sense to solicit volunteers to serve on a committee will sometimes try to dictate its leadership. This may cause people to keep away, or to resent your authoritarian approach.

Make clear in the beginning the scope of the committee's power. Few things will sour members more than imposing limits midway through a committee's lifetime. This is a

common reason for committee failure. The member who
drops out says it is because "We're wasting our time. Our
hands are tied." The feeling is a valid one if you've let the
group spend hours deliberating issues that you didn't want it
to consider, but neglected to mention.

Give the members credit. The work of the committee may be
a limited success. Those doing the work nonetheless deserve
recognition. You can't go wrong with occasional applause,
and it should encourage others to serve at a later date.

If you accept the premise that effective management is a
person-to-person, situational consideration, then you'll have
to agree that the leadership of a group constitutes one of the
most substantial challenges an executive must face. Not only
is a group composed of individual personalities, but
furthermore, each group has a personality of its own. Thus,
successful group leadership requires a full measure of the
manager's sensitivity, flexibility, and personal security.

chapter 10 Standing Out In Meetings

Managers find that a reputation for effectiveness in meetings boosts their promotability. Leadership and negotiation skills are highly visible. One watches a group-wise manager in action, then compares the manager who doesn't have the knack and thinks, "They're light-years apart."

There is a notable difference, but just mastering a relatively few key points can move you into the effective category and, since most organizations provide little or no training in group leadership and participation, you'll gain a competitive edge over your less skilled colleagues.

Observing the Group Process

Managers who complain about the time spent in meetings and the frequently disappointing results usually point to the way conferences are conducted—the *methods* of running the meetings. Or they cite the group's inability to decide what goals should be achieved, what they're really there to do—the *content*.

There is, however, a third factor in the success or failure of meetings, one which gets too little attention. Psychologists call it *process*, and define it as all the things that go on among people in a group. Though there is an almost infinite variety of interactions possible among people, some of those that occur at meetings are easily identifiable. Recognizing them, and developing the skills to deal with them, can be of major help in making your participation in conferences successful. This includes, of course, being able to assess your own role in the group and knowing what you do that helps or hinders the group in reaching the goal.

Take a look at the following frequently observed situations and behaviors, some effective, some obstructive. Being able to recognize them is an important first step in making you a skilled meeting participant.

Locking in. When you talk, try to avoid "locking in" on one person. It's very natural to notice someone in the group who shows apparent agreement with you by smiling or nodding, and then talk to that person, knowing that you will get some form of reinforcement. But you may be undermining your colleague's power to help you by causing him or her to be labeled as your ally. More important, by seeming to exclude others, you risk alienating them.

Rushing to defend. Don't rush to answer a question or defend your position against attack. Pause to make sure you really have all the necessary information about the other person's view. Sometimes your silence will lead your "attacker" to amplify the original statement, helping to clarify the issue. Or you may find that, while you're thinking, someone else will try to answer for you. That person's response may carry more weight than yours. Above all, don't interrupt someone who is challenging your views, even when you're sure he or she has missed your point. There's always the possibility that your associate is telling you something you ought to hear.

If a colleague openly or even angrily objects to what you are saying, listen carefully and look at the person. You are getting important feedback that may indicate where you have not performed effectively. If he or she becomes patently unfair, you may well find yourself defended by your colleagues—which is often much more effective than taking up the cudgel in your own behalf.

Conflict. Sharp, prolonged argument among a few members of the group can fog the matter under discussion and shut out constructive comments. If the people arguing are the group's dominant personalities or in authority, others at the meeting may draw back and become spectators. They may not realize that the disputants are sometimes as uncomfortable as everyone else, but don't know how to call a halt and save face at the same time.

If you sense that a feud is shutting off useful discussion or is creating bad feeling, try a suggestion like, "Why don't we get some comments from others about what you three have been talking about." Then look around the room, asking, "How does everyone else feel?" If you don't get a contribution immediately, make one of your own. When you see that someone else is interested, call on that individual for a response.

Domination. People who try to take over may not even be aware of what they are really doing. The would-be dominator may rationalize, "Well, I'm a person who likes to get things done. Let's cut through all this garbage and settle this thing."

The problem is that dominators frequently regard everything that doesn't conform to their views as garbage. And they are almost as frequently wrong.

If the people present are used to leveling with each other, if there's trust and a strong commitment to doing what's best for the whole group, you can confront the dominator. "Hey, I'm getting the feeling that you're ramrodding this meeting. Could you ease up so that everyone else can get a word in?"

Such a direct approach isn't always desirable, however. You don't want to start a time-consuming fight with a dominator. An alternate technique is to say, "Okay, I have a pretty good idea of where you are, but I haven't heard much from Neal or Betty, and I'm really interested in what they're thinking, too." Give the people who have been standing off a chance to speak out. The dominator will usually give in, not wanting to be seen as a dictator.

Withdrawal. In meetings that are highly competitive, full of strong personalities, some people get squashed. They sit back in silence. The more vocal participants get so involved in what is going on that they don't notice. Sometimes they don't care.

Yet people who sit it out may have important contributions to make. They can easily come to feel that no one cares about their ideas and bring that attitude to future meetings. Even worse, they will probably be less committed to carrying out the decisions arrived at by more articulate colleagues.

Sometimes someone calls on the silent person in an unintentionally accusing fasion. "We haven't heard from you, Sam." Not only does this seem to imply that Sam has been shirking, it also seems to carry the message, "You'd better come up with something good." A better approach would be, "Sam, you've been looking very thoughtful. I'd like to hear what's been running through your mind. That is, if you'd care to." That gives Sam an out. If Sam talks and gets interrupted, come back to him as soon as you have a chance.

Shutting off. There seem to be an almost infinite variety of ways to gag a member of the group. The most common method of shutting someone off is simply to interrupt, either with an answer that may (or may not) be related to what the person is saying, or with a statement that clearly conveys, "You're wrong," or "That's ridiculous." A more subtle but just as damaging way is to take some aspect of the person's point and turn it into a joke. By the time everyone gets through laughing, what was said has lost its impact.

The danger is that, although the shutting off is usually unintentional, the participant interrupted will not only drop the point but will abstain from any further activity within the group.

You can rescue the situation. As soon as possible, ask the person who has been shut off a question like this. "Did you get a chance to finish, Charlie? Was there anything you wanted to add?" You may even wish to let him know you think he was shut off. "I have a feeling that we didn't give Charlie a chance to finish his point, and I'd like to hear him out."

Making judgments. Her face is red. Her voice comes in spurts and is considerably louder than usual. But ask her what she is so hot under the collar about and watch what happens. She will probably deny that she is angry, and in fact she may not really know she is. She then drops the issue she was arguing before and begins to argue about whether or not she is angry.

You don't have to ignore the other's behavior, but emphasize what effect that behavior is having on you rather than labeling it as "defensive" or whatever. If you think someone is upset, tell him you think he is. Or that he appears that way to you. When you put it that way, there really is little or nothing to argue about. The other person can hardly dispute the way you feel, and he doesn't have to defend himself against some general accusation. He can simply say to you, "I don't agree with your perception of me."

Analyzing behavior. The temptation is strong in many people to play amateur analyst, to tell colleagues not only what they are doing but why they are doing it. "You're overcompensating," or "You're just getting back at me for what I did last month," or "You're projecting." Any or all of these might be true in a given case, but no one except the person being analyzed can know for sure, and he or she may not be easy to convince. While you try, the subject of the meeting is switched to the siding.

Missing the target. "That's not what I said," retorts A heatedly to B's interpretation (or rebuttal) of the point that she has just made. Everything in the meeting stops while A repeats her original point, which she probably can't do accurately now because she feels defensive and uptight. "You didn't listen to me," is a similar rejoinder and also a red flag to indicate that B's argument has missed the target—that is, A's point.

The problem is that most of us don't always listen well, or that our biases prevent us from being able to analyze

objectively what is being said. We waste time, rebutting
points that were never made. One way to keep things on the
track and avoid the suspicion of unfairness is to repeat
another's point, and get the originator's agreement that you
understand what has been said, before you respond to it.

If it is your own point that is being misunderstood,
especially if you feel hemmed in by several challenges and
objections, get help from others. For example, "I guess I
haven't done justice to this," or "I guess I haven't made this
clear. Can someone else here help me out?" The point is, place
the blame for the lack of understanding (if that's what it is) on
yourself. You may be surprised to find how much help in
clarifying or in closing gaps you'll get. Even if this does not
resolve the situation, you'll get the pressure off yourself for the
moment. It's hard to think clearly when you feel trapped.

Observing group process doesn't have to be an involved
deal. Usually it just takes a bit of attention, but that "bit" can
really pay off in terms of a meeting's success. And you don't
have to be the conference leader to be aware of process. Just
ask yourself these questions:

What's going on at the moment? Is anyone preventing others
from talking? Or showing more anger than the issue really
warrants?

*Is what is going on helpful to the group or a hindrance, or
neither?* Process-observing doesn't mean looking solely for
the bad things. Some participants should be encouraged in
what they are doing—for example, supporting the chances for
others to present their ideas. If something is happening that is
potentially destructive to the group's goals, however, ask the
next question:

*Is the potentially harmful activity so prolonged or serious that
action should be taken to head it off?* If not, let the matter go
without a fuss. If so, try to get the group heading in the right
direction, preferably without embarrassing anyone. As a first
step, sound out other members of the group as to how they see

what is happening. It's a bad moment when one person breaks into a discussion to say, "I don't see what this has to do with what we're supposed to be doing," then finds that others disagree strongly with that assessment.

At the same time, you can make positive contributions to the group process:

Emphasize areas of agreement. There are areas of agreement that you can call to the attention of the group. Even if these are minor matters, the group will develop a sense that it is getting on with the job, and it will be easier to move to a resolution of the larger issues. And you will appear insightful.

Include everyone. Make sure you get response from all the members of the group. From time to time ask, "Is this clear to everyone?" If there is a general lack of response, you'd be well advised to keep questioning frequently. Eventually someone will speak up and possibly give you a lead as to what may be troubling several participants.

Be prepared to concede. Be realistic about the concessions you can afford to make. Sometimes your willingness to give up a minor point—"Of course, we can clear with you on this"—can make all the difference in getting acceptance of your major proposition. Know what you can afford, and cannot afford, to yield.

Ask for a decision. Don't hesitate to ask for action on a proposal or decision. This is one of the best ways to smoke out any hidden objectives or reservations that otherwise might not appear until after the meeting, if then.

Listen. Many people don't. You're not, if you are rehearsing what you are going to say while another person is speaking. You listen to yourself instead of to the other person and, by doing so, may wind up missing some important information.

Look for possibilities. Suppose that someone has just given a presentation or offered an extensive proposal. There will be some listeners who concentrate on finding fault, especially if the area under consideration is one in which they feel pretty knowledgeable.

A more constructive response than trying to look good by finding fault is to focus on the possibilites in the proposal and define them in terms of organizational objectives. In today's results-oriented world, making an idea workable is usually considered more valuable than showing why it won't work.

Neutralizing the No

No discussion of behavioral obstacles to a group's success would be complete without talking about the power of a negative response. You've probably felt it when you were sponsoring an idea or recommending a course of action about which others were unsure.

It's discouraging but true that people seem not to demand the same justification for a *nay* that they do for an *aye*. It doesn't have to be an out-and-out *no*. It usually isn't. "Let's hold off on this" or "I think we ought to go slowly" or "We should take another look at that one aspect" is often the same as "No."

In the face of uncertainty, it is perfectly understandable to hold off making a decision, to take another look. And it's just as human to want to be able to ally oneself with the "I told you so" side if the venture proves to be unworkable.

Nonetheless, understanding why people respond so quickly to a negative voice is small comfort to you when you want positive action taken on a project that is close to you. And of course there is always the possibility that a negative or delaying vote is justified.

There are steps you can consider when confronted by delay or failure to act:

Clarify the risk. In making a risky decision, no one wants to be taxed with having made a mistake. But there are situations when a mistake is less deadly than in others. In some cases, if the decision proves to be a mistake, it will hardly bankrupt you. Or if the decision is not made, there will be searching questions from up the line as to why no action was taken. Put the decision in perspective. Show that the stakes are not as high as people seem to think, that the consequences of not making a positive decision could be worse for all concerned than taking a step that falls short of success.

Sell the benefits. "Okay," you might point out, "perhaps this may fail, and some people will be a little unhappy because we decided to risk it. But we'll get some data we couldn't obtain any other way." You may, in fact, have more tangible benefits to offer from a go-ahead decision. But the point is that whatever good things could come out of a risky decision should be reemphasized in case some members of the group didn't recognize their value the first time around.

Neutralize the challenge to you. Sometimes in pushing for a project you can anticipate that opposition will come not because someone disagrees with your ideas, but because he or she objects to your leadership in presenting the idea. Generally you can recognize this opposition for what it is; you have probably encountered it before. When you find yourself faced with such a challenge to your leadership, work to get the discussion into a different arena. For example, you might say, "I guess everyone can see how Mark and I feel. So I suggest we hear more from the people who haven't said much." If you can't be the leader, then multiply the leadership.

Call attention to obstructive behavior. The person who is throwing up opposition to a positive decision—or to any decision—may or may not be aware of the obstructive role he or she is playing. In some situations, you may want to put some straightforward questions. Why the pressure to hold off? How do the dangers outweigh the benefits? What's the worst that can happen if a positive decision is made? Or with a different person it might be sufficient to say, "Look, I think you are closing out the chances to consider this fairly."

Pushing without Dominating

If you really want to be a hero, rescue a meeting that isn't going anywhere. People quibble over semantics, divert the discussion with anecdotes, ramble interminably. It is definitely time for someone to provide some leadership. You have strong, clear ideas about how the group ought to move and in what direction, and now is the moment for you to take things in hand. Right?

Well, maybe yes. Maybe no. If you are chairman, you don't want to look as if you are imposing your will—that can lead to rebellion. If you are merely a member of the group, giving the impression that you are trying to take over may be resented by your peers as well as by the leader you try to replace. Later, when the chairman has acquired the necessary strength, he may find ways to repay you for that threat to his authority and image.

Nonetheless, when a conference is drifting there are acceptable ways to get it moving toward its goals. It all depends on your approach.

Be patient. You may assume nothing is happening because that's the way it looks. Yet people who are not accustomed to working together usually need a while to take each other's measure. A certain amount of noncommittal, cautious rambling helps them get to know one another and develop a feeling for their various positions on issues that may arise. The content of such talk may not be significant, but if it results in group cohesiveness, the time is well spent.

This initial period also gives you a chance to discover any currents that may be developing apart from the stated purpose of the meeting. For example, one person may be hoping to use the meeting to revive a proposal on a different subject that has been turned down previously. As we'll see later, such "hidden agendas" are often present in meetings.

Be low-key. You want the tacit consent of the group to step in. You can say something like, "I wonder if I could throw some ideas out and see what kinds of reactions you have."

Getting the group's consent to your efforts to move it along does several things. It encourages everyone to listen carefully; also, you may get instant help from those who have been silently praying somebody would do something. If people still aren't ready to move on to the substantial matters, you'll get a signal that this isn't the time for you to push.

Stay simple and basic. Introduce any ideas you have in a brief, general form. Don't give people the impression that you've already worked everything out, that you were simply waiting for the right moment to take over. You can always flesh out the picture as others begin to respond to your suggestions.

Look for help. To avoid the appearance of imposing your will on the group, let others discuss what you've offered. Confine your role to that of clarifying your ideas when others seem unclear about them.

Leave the back door open. Many people tend to press hard at this time, to argue and try to ramrod their way. But why bring the issue to the point of possible rejection? If you can back off, you can regroup your forces and come in again when there seems to be a vacuum.

The person who, early in the meeting, tries to dominate the session by talking a great deal, pushing for early votes, pressing his or her own proposals, and showing impatience may not detect any serious antagonism at the time. In fact, if the meeting is meandering, other members who are bored or restless will often welcome the person who steps in to shape things up. But when the group members have developed more confidence in their individual abilities to work together, a backlash can develop against anyone they see as trying to dominate the group.

The person who began as a hero winds up as a villain. Whatever the person's intentions, he or she is seen as a dominator, a manipulator, and a string-puller. People may suspect an effort to force them into actions they aren't ready to take.

When people feel they have been pressured into something, they lack commitment. They don't feel responsible for carrying out the project. The strong-minded person with innovative ideas who is tempted to provide leadership when it seems to be sorely needed would be wise to remember that people will not welcome anything that looks like an attempt to do their thinking for them.

Dealing with the Hidden Agenda

Occasionally there will be individual or group interactions seemingly based on issues that are not, strictly speaking, the stated business of the meeting. One participant spends a lot of time countering another person's proposals, until it seems as if nothing the latter can offer is acceptable. Or two people in the group constantly reinforce each other's contributions until you suspect they are trying to form a power bloc. Still another co-worker vehemently argues against any idea that suggests existing procedures be changed.

Confronted with such activity, you may suspect a hidden or personal agenda. Both are brought into the conference room by one or more participants, and they may run counter to the formal or stated agenda. For example, the person who opposes everything his co-worker says may be getting even for something the co-worker has done or said outside the meeting, even if settling the score means frustrating the group's progress. The "mutual admiration society" may indeed have agreed beforehand on ways to dominate the discussion. The person who resists any changes may be thinking, "If I allow this, I'll see my job disappear."

Thus the personal or hidden agenda may be either rational or emotional in character. Sometimes it makes an appearance and then disappears, quickly and harmlessly. At other times it may seriously hamper the progress of the group.

A covert agenda is sometimes very hard to deal with, but here are some suggestions:

Regard personal and hidden agendas as natural. Any time you convene a group of people who take partisan positions or who have experienced conflict with one another, you can expect informal or covert agendas. They're a natural phenomenon of the group process.

Don't rush to take action. Most covert agendas will surface in the early part of a meeting, and often they'll be taken care of without special effort. The manager who wants the next management meeting to be held in Boston so that he can take a few days off to hit the ski slopes in New Hampshire will be told that travel restrictions necessitate that the site be near Philadelphia. People who rush to head off what they see as personal agendas are open to the charge that they are preventing the meeting from moving ahead.

Don't ignore the obstructive agenda. If the meeting has ground to a halt because of a confrontation between two people or because one person is being domineering, you have the choice of sitting there and letting the frustration build or doing something. Don't expect the leader or other participants to know what to do. They may be as frustrated as you, and less certain about what to do. One thing you can do is say to the chairman or others, "I'm having a problem tying this in with what we're supposed to be doing," or, "Am I alone in feeling that we're not making much progress toward our goal?" It's usually a good idea to ask for others' opinions or help in resolving the problem. You may find that others are happy to jump to your support.

One word of caution: It's not wise to announce that you think someone in the group has been responsible for getting the session off the track. A head-on assault will often bring a counterattack, and the person accused will spend much time defending the obstructive actions. Be tentative and open to correction when you suggest that progress has been slowed or sidetracked.

There will be some under-the-table agendas that you suspect but find hard to label as such. Some steps you can take to bring them to the surface:

Let them rise. If you think there are subterranean forces at work, say, "I wonder if we've said everything we think about this. Why don't we take a little more time to make sure that everyone has had a say." Sometimes this encouragement will persuade a member of the group to open up when he or she has been circumspect.

Don't force. If the persons involved want to conceal what is really going on in their minds or between them, they'll resist any overt attempts to make them come clean, and such attempts may further disrupt the meeting. In one meeting a frustrated manager tried to embarrass the people he felt were forcing their own agendas on the others by saying, "What I hear is some people grinding their axes." Not only did progress stop on working out the hidden agendas, but any forward movement toward the stated goals stopped as well. The people involved in the covert activity fell silent and refused to participate in the formal discussion.

Try to get around the obstruction. Switch the discussion to another aspect of the business at hand, if possible, suggesting a return to the disputed issue after a rest. In the case of dominant personalities, try to get others involved in the discussion. To get the discussion back into the mainstream, try formulating questions that you would like others to help you answer, or soliciting the views of others who are not participating. In short, create some legitimate competition for those indulging their personal agendas.

Helping the Conference Clam
Some people don't participate freely in group situations. They clam up. They constitute an unused resource. Sometimes these people really do want to open up, but just can't seem to find the will or the way.

You can help. Your help will probably be effective and welcome even if you aren't the formal leader of the group. You will, of course, be exercising useful informal leadership if you bring the clam into the deliberations. Some recommendations:

Prepare the clam. Tell the clam of a subject that is bound to come up, one on which he or she can talk knowledgeably. Let the reticent person know that you'll be asking for an opinion or a short presentation.

Refer to the clam's specialty or experience. "Didn't you do some work in this area a couple of years back, Sheila?" Or,

"Jim has some opinions in this area, because he was talking to me the other day about it. Jim, would you mind repeating what you said to me?"

Supply questions. Phrase questions that call for specific responses. "How does this emergency breakdown procedure look to you?" or, "Jerry, do you think we could live with this service policy? How do you think it will stack up in cost?"

Take the contributions seriously. Recognize, however briefly, the clam's remarks. One way is to relate what has been said to your own thinking. "What Peggy says is something I've been wondering about." Or comment on the value of the clam's statement. "That's something I hadn't thought about."

Nothing, however, can be more damaging to the clam than to praise something he or she has said because it was said, not because it had any merit. If it doesn't have merit, go on to something else. A recognition of merit where merit doesn't exist will cause others to be annoyed—and less respectful of both you and the clam.

Assuming that the clam's remarks do have merit, however, in time others will recognize what you are doing, and will add their encouragement and reinforcement. Not only will the clam become a more useful member of the group, but you will be seen as a person who makes it possible for human resources to be more fully utilized.

Confronting the Hog

Chances are good that you've been in meetings dominated by one person. Sometimes the domination is intentional; the person wants to run things. Other times the person may have been unable to organize thoughts beforehand and so cannot speak concisely. He or she may ramble or talk compulsively. Unfortunately, in many groups these people don't find out how others feel about their obnoxious behavior. Or the dominator, the true hog, may actually feel reinforced and encouraged by the group.

In most cases, the worst thing you can do is to do nothing.

When you have a hog in the meeting, the group needs help.
The hog also needs help.

Here are some suggestions for limiting or putting pressure
on the hog:

Insist on hearing from others. "Okay," you might say to the
hog, "I have a fairly good idea where you stand. Now I'd like
to find out how others think." If you have to, call upon others
by name. "Jim, how do you feel about what Carla has been
saying?"

Ask for clarification. In the case of the rambler, interrupt
when you're not sure what is being said or where the rambler
is going. "I'm not sure, Terry, what that last statement means.
Can you explain?" Or, "Are you saying, Gene, that you don't
think we can deliver? Why do you think that way?"

Look for minor points to concede. Surprisingly often, a
person who takes up the group time is sticking on minor
points—and others don't realize it. The hog may be unable to
deal with the major or more complicated issues. He or she
may be looking for recognition. People fail to see what is
happening and get into involved confrontations. If you look
carefully, you may find that what is being elaborated is in
reality not worth the effort. "Oh, what I understand, John, is
that you think we should move the deadline from Tuesday to
Wednesday every third month. Is that right?" You may find
that is exactly what he is spending so much time talking
about—and that you can grant the concession and get back to
major points.

Plead time pressure. This is not always the most desirable way
to limit someone, but it may be necessary. "Hey, we have to
break up in twenty minutes, so I think we ought to go around
the table and get everybody's last comments."

Keep in mind that, with the compulsive talker, the
monopolizer, or the rambler, no one-time action is going to be
effective. You are aiming for a change of behavior—and that
takes time. Even on a one-time basis, you hope at least to

increase the effectiveness of the hog and reduce the frustrating effect he or she may have on you and the group.

* * * * * * * * * * * * *

Each group has its own personality, created in large part by the behavior of the individuals in the group as well as by the task the group is expected to perform. As a skilled executive, whether you are the formal leader or are exercising informal and spontaneous leadership skills, you have considerable influence over the dynamics of the meeting. Your own behavior can contribute much to the effectiveness of the group in reaching its objective. And what you do to help the group to operate well can call attention to you.

Index

action up the line, getting, 108-10
adult ego state, 60
agenda
  covert, 196-98
  hidden, 196-98
  personal, 196-98
alcohol problems, avoiding responsibility for, 55-56
alcoholic lunches, 55
anger
  concealed, 129
  expressed unexpectedly, 130-31
  tolerated, 129
anger at you, subordinates', 38-39
applicants, job
  interviewing, 160-62
  using stress with, 162-64
attack, dealing with a public, 88-90
attack by a subordinate, countering, 38-39
attention
  getting an unwilling audience's, 91-93
  getting the boss', 103-06
  obstacles to, 104

bad news, delivering, 155
battle, willingness to do, 129
behavior conditioning, 9
behavior
  criticism of, 149-50
  nonlogical, 34

reinforcing the, 9, 59-61
behaviors
  analyzing group, 189
  common group, 186-90
boss
  being negative with the, 119-21
  challenging a decision of the, 119-21
  complaining to the, 121-23
  delegating to the, 107-08
  evaluating the, 98-100
  getting attention of the, 103-06
  looking good to the new, 115-19
  praising the, 102-03
  protecting yourself in a conflict with the, 123-24
  supporting the, 100-02
  taking the measure of the, 98-100
  the backsliding, 100
  the mobile, 99
  the shelf-sitting, 99-100
  using clout with the, 124-26
  using power on the, 124-26
bulletin board, the departmental, 102

challenging a decision of the boss, 119-21
change, measuring subordinates' feelings about, 27-29
climate, work, 2

cognitive dissonance, 177
collaboration, 93-96
committee, getting results
    from a, 183-84
communicating
    as subordinates' responsi-
        bility, 22
    improving horizontal, 92
    in an interview, 160-62
    in a subordinate's office,
        157-58
communications, pitfalls in,
    26
competition, 93
    among managers, 44
complainer, dealing with the
    continual, 62-64
complaining to the boss, 121-
    23
compliments for the boss,
    102-103
conditioning, behavior, 9
conference
    clam, 198-99
    hog, 199-201
conflict
    admitting, 128-31
    as a sign of vigor, 131
    avoiding suppression of,
        132-35
    benefiting from, 131-32
    group, 187
    in public, 88-90
    personality-oriented, 139
    problem-centered, 139
    protecting yourself in oth-
        ers', 142-44
    resolution, 136-38
    status in, 135

suppressing, 127-28
using the confrontation
    technique in resolving,
    135-36
with the boss, protecting
    yourself in a, 123-24
Conflict, Decision and Dis-
    sonance, 177
confrontation technique in
    resolving conflict, 135-36
consensus decisions, 179
content, group, 185
conveying your expectations
    of subordinates'
    performance, 1-4, 159
cooperation, 93
counseling, personal, 37
covert agenda, 196-98
criticism
    as recognition, 150-51
    best time for, 155
    broadside, 147-48
    by phone, 153-54
    humor as, 67-68
    justified, 112, 114
    learning from, 150-51
    mixing with praise, 151-53
    of a subordinate, 145
    of behavior, 149-50
    of performance, 64-67
    phone vs. pen, 153-54
    place to give, 157
    playing psychoanalyst in,
        148-49
    risky techniques of, 145-49
    sandbagging technique of,
        146-47
    sandwich technique of,
        145-46, 151-52, 153

using labels in, 149-50

decisions, making firm, 176-79
defending yourself from a subordinate's attack, 38-39
defensive subordinate, 64-67
delegate, getting the boss to, 106-07
delegating to the boss, 107-08
delegation upward, 108
delivering bad news, 155
disagreement, suppression of, 132-35
discussion in meetings, developing good, 175-76
dissonance, cognitive, 177
domination of a group, 187-88
drinking problems, avoiding responsibility for a subordinate's, 55-56
dropping in on a subordinate, 157-58

ego state, adult, 60
employee
countering an attack by an, 38-39
criticizing a, 145
failure of a, 5
the defensive, 64-67
the obsolescent, 41-45
the temperamental, 61-62
toning down a gifted, 61-62
with a past, 70-72
employee's

anger at you, 38-39
recovery from a setback, 49-53
employees
doing the work of, 68-70
enhancing the motivation of, 4-5
feuding, 138-40
importance of, how they feel about, 16
older, 47
participation of in planning, 26
performance of, 1-3
personal objectives of, 8-9
personal problems of, 74-75
employees'
opinions of you, 31-34
perceptions of you, 31-32
encouraging employees without promising, 159-60
evaluating the boss, 98-100
excusaholic, working with an, 53-55
expectations of employees' performance, conveying your, 1-4, 159

failure
of meetings, 171-72
of subordinates, 51
Federal Mediation and Conciliation Service, 136, 138
feedback, 10, 31, 32, 33
management of, 27
feelings
accepting, 36
disguising as fact, 35

hearing, 34-37
Festinger, Leon, 177
feud
  deciding whether to intervene in, 138-40
  heading off interdepartmental, 141-42
feuding employees, 138-40
firing, 18
  covering up a, 164-65

game ethic, 135
gifted subordinate, toning down a, 61-62
goals, matching with subordinates', 43
goal-setting, 5-8
group
  behaviors, analyzing, 189
  behaviors, common, 186-90
  conflict, 187
  confronting the conference hog in a, 199-201
  content, 185
  dealing with a hidden agenda in a, 196-98
  domination of a, 187-88
  effective leadership in a, 179-182
  getting results from a, 183-84
  helping the conference clam in a, 198-99
  leadership functions in a, 171-72
  methods, 185
  premature solutions in a, 172, 176

presentation, 167-68
process, 185-92
pushing to get results in a, 194-96
silencing members of a, 182-83

harmony, excessive, 131
Herzberg, Frederick, 13
hidden agenda, 196-98
horizontal communication, improving, 92
humor
  as criticism, 67-68
  as put-down, 85
  at your expense, 67-68

ideas
  getting subordinates' about yours, 29-31
  in a group, generating, 173-75
importance, how subordinates feel about their, 16
information, lapses in, 25
interdepartmental negotiation, 81
interviews
  communicating in, 160-62
  using a professional in, 163-64
  using stress in, 162-64
interviewing job applicants, 160-62
intervening in a feud, 138-40
isolation, avoiding, 21-25

Jay, Antony, 42
job applicants

interviewing, 160-62
using stress with, 162-64
joking, de-fanging the, 82-85
joking relationships, 83

key people, recognizing, 16-17
Kick Me game, 60

labels, using in criticism, 149-50
leadership
effective group, 179-82
functions in a group, 171-72
task force, 179-82
listen, getting the boss to, 103-06
listening, obstacles to, 104

MBO, *see Management by Objectives*
Management and Machiavelli, 42
Management by Objectives, 5-8, 44, 102
management style, 42
managerial competition, 44
managerial obsolescence, 41-45
managing news, 25-27
meetings
choosing the right size for, 172-73
developing a good discussion in a, 173-75
getting ideas for, 173-75
failure of, 171-72
mentor, 113-15

method, group, 185
motivation
effect of weeding out on, 17-19
enhancing employees', 1, 4-5

needler, dealing with a, 68
negotiation, between departments, 81
new boss, looking good to a, 115-19
news, delivering bad, 155
news, managing, 25-27
no, the power of in a group, 192-93
nonlogical behavior, 34

objectives, employees' personal, 8-9
Objectives, Management by, 5-8, 44, 102
Objectives, Relationships by, 136-38
obsolescence
managerial, 41-45
manifestations of, 42-43
obstacles to attention, 104
office affair, 72-74
older employees, 47
opinions, of you, subordinates', 31-34
organization man, 46

partiality, showing, 12-16
participation of subordinates in planning, 26
peacemaking, 133-34
peers

dealing with an attack by, 88-90
dealing with put-downs by, 85-87
getting the attention of, 90-93
joking relationships with, 82-85
negotiating with, 81
partnership with, 93-96
solving problems with, 77-81
winning over, 81-82
perception, 135
faulty role, 45-47
perceptions, of you by subordinates, 31-32
performance
conveying expectations of subordinates', 1-4, 159
counseling, 64
criticism of, 64-67
standards, 18-19
subordinates', 1-3
personality-oriented conflict, 139
phone, criticizing by, 153-54
pitfalls in communicating, 26
positive reinforcement, 9-11, 103
praise, 11-12
praising the boss, 102-03
presentation
group, 167-68
to the boss, making a, 125
planning a, 167-69
problem
defining the, 79
employee's personal, 74-75

problem-centered conflict, 139
problems
avoiding responsibility for alcohol, 55-56
solving interdepartmental, 77-81
process, group, 185-92
professional in interviews, using a, 163-64
promises, making inadvertent, 159-60
promotability, visibility as essential to, 100-02
protégé, protecting yourself as a, 113-15
public attack, 88-90
publicizing oneself, 165-67
put-down
handling the, 85-87
humor as, 85
put-downs, avoiding making, 155-57

RBO, *see Relationships by Objectives*
raise, asking for a, 110-13
recognition
as motivator, 9, 12, 15
criticism as, 150-51
of key people, 16-17
recovery, from a setback, subordinate's, 49-53
reinforcement, positive, 9-11, 103
reinforcing the wrong behavior, 59-61
Relationships by Objectives, 136-38
relationships, joking, 83

resistance to your ideas, 90-93

resolving conflict, 135-38
  using confrontation technique in, 135-36
results, from a group, getting, 183-84
retiree, on-the-job, 47-49
reward, 11, 13, 14, 15, 16, 66
role, faulty perception of, 45-47
romance, office, 72-74
Rotter, Julian, 4

sandbagging technique of criticism, 146-47
sandwich technique of criticism, 145-46, 151-52, 153
setback, a subordinate's recovery from a, 49-53
setting goals, 5-8
sex in the office, 72-74
size of group, choosing the right, 172-73
Skinner, B.F., 9
social learning theory, 4-5
sponsor, 113-15
state, adult ego, 60
status in conflict, 135
stress in interviewing, 162-64
subordinate
  countering an attack by a, 38-39
  criticizing a, 145
  failure of a, 5
  the defensive, 64-67
  the obsolescent, 41-45
  the temperamental, 61-62
  toning down a gifted, 61-62

with a past, 70-72
subordinate's
  anger at you, 38-39
  recovery from a setback, 49-53
subordinates
  doing the work of, 68-70
  enhancing the motivation of, 4-5
  feuding, 138-40
  importance of, how they feel about, 16
  older, 47
  participation of in planning, 26
  performance of, 1-3
  personal objectives of, 8-9
  personal problems of, 74-75
subordinates'
  opinions of you, 31-34
  perceptions of you, 31-32
supporting the boss, 100-02
suppressing conflict, 127-128
suppression
  of conflict, avoiding, 132-35
  of disagreement, 132-35

Tactful Silence game, 29
task force leadership, 179-82
team maintenance, 41
Transactional Analysis, 59, 60
termination, avoiding embarrassment in announcing, 164-65

upward delegation, 108

vigor, conflict as a sign of,
   131
visibility, as essential to
   promotability, 100-02

weeding out, the effect on

motivation of, 17-19
winning gracefully, 81-82
work climate, 2
wunderkind, dealing with
   the, 61-62